modern retro
table style

modern retro
table style

living with mid-century tableware

RYLAND
PETERS
& SMALL
LONDON NEW YORK

madeleine marsh

with photography by **thomas stewart**

Designer Luis Peral-Aranda
Senior editor Sophie Bevan
Location research manager Kate Brunt
Production Patricia Harrington
Art director Gabriella Le Grazie
Publishing director Alison Starling

Stylist Siri Hills
Period props researched and sourced by Luis Peral-Aranda

First published in the USA in 2002
by Ryland Peters & Small, Inc.
519 Broadway, 5th Floor
New York NY 10012
www.rylandpeters.com

10 9 8 7 6 5 4 3 2 1

Text © Madeleine Marsh 2002
Design and photographs © Ryland Peters & Small 2002

Printed and bound in China.

Library of Congress Cataloguing-in-Publication Data

Marsh, Madeleine, 1960–
   Modern retro table style : living with mid-century modern tableware /
by Madeleine Marsh.
      p. cm.
   ISBN 1-84172-273-1
   1. Table setting and decoration. I. Title.

TX879 .M38 2002
642`.7--dc21

CONTENTS

INTRODUCTION

The aim of
this book is to explore the changing
tastes in tableware from the 1940s to the 1970s,
and to show how these vintage objects can be stylishly
incorporated into the modern interior. One of the joys of collecting
retro tableware, is the pleasure of living with it. This is not a book about
precious antiques, frozen in time and locked away in a display cabinet. Whilst
some of the period pieces shown are purely decorative, many more are still
performing the ordinary household tasks for which they were created, perhaps half a
century ago. Standing alongside contemporary products on kitchen countertops, dining-
room tables, and living-room sideboards, these are collectibles that are used and actively
enjoyed. Though they might have been designed in the past, they work in the present—living
proof that good design is timeless. The book is divided into two parts. The first sets tableware
in its period context. It looks at the major media—ceramics, glass, metalware, wood, plastic
—and explores postwar developments in pattern, shape, and color. But this is not just a
history of the applied arts. With the end of World War II, came a huge period of change.
The objects displayed chart the move from '40s austerity, to '50s affluence. They reflect
the ephemeral Pop styles of the urban, swinging '60s and the brown and oatmeal
countrified look of the back-to-nature '70s. By its very nature, tableware tells
the story of the people who used it: what they ate and drank, how they
decorated their homes, how they entertained, their fashions,
aspirations, and lifestyles. These everyday items—mugs,
plates, knives, and forks—provide not just a
decorative picture of their

times, but

also a social history and a hands-on,

three-dimensional link with the past. The second part

of this book goes into present-day houses and apartments

where retro tableware is used and displayed. Every home tells its own

decorative story. We look at the effect that new and exotic foodstuffs had on

the domestic tabletop. We meet the Scandinavian designers who exported teak

furnishings and rational Modernism to homes across the world. We witness the birth of

the modern kitchen with its shiny chrome appliances. And we chart the extravagance

of '60s fashions, from Italian space-age plastics to British Pop-art products. Contrasting with

these glowing psychedelic interiors, is the more natural and neutral look of a country-style

kitchen, with its bare wood and '70s handcrafted pottery: a modern return to our rural past. In

these living rooms, kitchens, and dining rooms, tableware is included from across the world,

reflecting the global nature of postwar shopping. Furnishing and decoration encompasses a

variety of tastes and reflects both the past and the present. However, these are not museum

settings or time capsules, but real homes where vintage and contemporary pieces are combined.

Purist collectors might insist on an original American food-mixer or a period Arne Jacobsen

kitchen chair, but equally some of these objects have never gone out of production. In

some instances (such as electrical kitchen appliances), whilst you might want a

period look, you might not want old equipment, and a modern version of

a vintage design can provide the perfect and practical solution. The

accent here is not to recreate the past, but to live with it in

the present, drawing on a range of periods, places,

objects, and influences to create a uniquely

personal style.

ELEMENTS OF THE RETRO TABLETOP

01MATERIALS | 02COLORS | 03SHAPES | 04PATTERNS

CERAMICS

Once wartime restrictions were lifted, the demand for ceramics boomed. In the U.S., industrial ceramic designers such as Eva Zeisel and Russel Wright were pioneering new shapes and colors in everyday ware. Inspired by their work, Finnish designer Kaj Franck and the Midwinter factory in Britain also created some of the most innovative tableware of the '50s, designed to meet the needs of a new generation of homeowners.

Iroquois Casual China designed by Russel Wright in 1946 came in mix-and-match colors, many named after food (sugar white, lettuce green, ripe apricot). Some shades, such as lemon yellow and parsley green, were withdrawn earlier than others, making them harder to find today.

ABOVE **Reflecting the rise in popularity of instant coffee and the teabag, the mug took over from the cup and saucer. These were made by the British firm Hornsea (established in 1949), who achieved huge success in the '60s and '70s with their mass-produced pottery that nevertheless retained a handmade country feel.**

ABOVE RIGHT **Kaj Franck's Kilta range was produced in 1953 for Arabia in five mix-and-match glazes—white, black, green, blue, and yellow. The waisted glass carafe was also designed by Franck circa 1955, and came in different colors.**

BELOW **These large pottery vases were made in 1955 by the French ceramicist Georges Jouve.**

Russel Wright's American Modern dinnerware, which retailed over 80 million pieces, introduced rimless plates and curvaceous streamlined pots to countless American homes in the '40s and '50s. In 1946, he created another bestseller with his Iroquois Casual China, featuring oven-to-table ware perfect for the kitchen-diner. Like American Modern, Iroquois was produced in different colors that the housewife could mix and match as she expanded her china along with her family. Wright's mix-and-match tableware was a major influence on Kaj Franck. His Kilta line, designed for Arabia in 1953, came in clear coordinating colors and simple standardized shapes. Stackable, affordable, and multifunctional, Kilta was the answer for those living in apartments or small houses and embracing an informal—and servantless—lifestyle.

Alongside this focus on mass production, there was a growing interest in individual craftsmanship. Major commercial factories, such as Gustavsberg in Sweden and Poole in England, also ran artistic studios where designers experimented with extravagant organic shapes, hand-painted colors, and new textures. In the '60s, small, independent potteries flourished, and fashionable urban shops, from Williams-Sonoma in San Francisco to Habitat in London, sold traditional French country earthenware.

Ceramic tableware reflected the postwar revolution in food and drink: the introduction of new products, foreign foods, and more relaxed eating habits. Perhaps the ultimate symbol of this new informality was the mug. Decorated with anything from abstract patterns to political slogans, mugs could be mixed, without having to match at all.

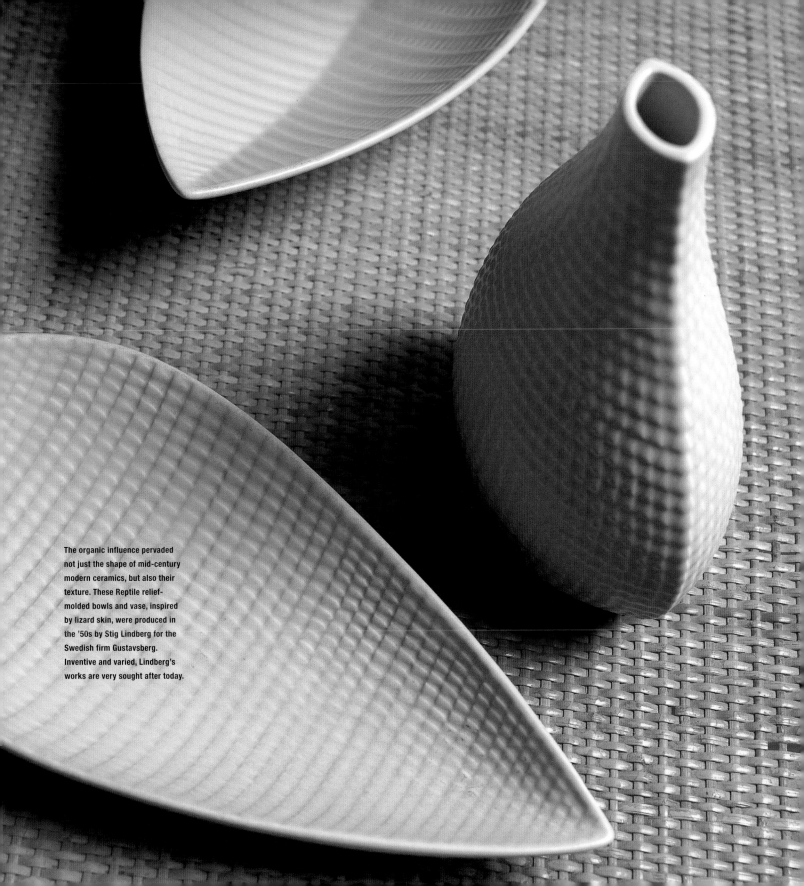

The organic influence pervaded
not just the shape of mid-century
modern ceramics, but also their
texture. These Reptile relief-
molded bowls and vase, inspired
by lizard skin, were produced in
the '50s by Stig Lindberg for the
Swedish firm Gustavsberg.
Inventive and varied, Lindberg's
works are very sought after today.

Glassware from different periods can be mixed and matched without losing a cohesive retro feel. Here amber glass—a '70s favorite—appears in many forms, including a clear Holmegaard bottle vase—or "Gulvase," as they were called—and modern stemware designed by Bowles and Linares which comes in two parts—a round-based vessel nestling in an elegant stand. Their elongated shapes fit perfectly with the tall vintage pieces.

MATERIALS

GLASS

Italy and Northern Europe dominated decorative glass design in the '50s and '60s. For centuries, the island of Murano in Venice had been a major center of glassmaking. Reviving ancient ornamental techniques, Venetian glassmaker Paolo Venini produced his famous series of handkerchief vases, folding squares of free-blown glass like napkins, and creating one of the most distinctive and most imitated shapes of the '50s.

Italian glass was noted for its brilliant color and bold, fanciful shapes at every level of the market, from the finest art glass to low-cost decorative ware. Minor workshops catered for the tourist trade, turning out multicolored glass fish and multi-layered sommerso ashtrays, a favorite on the '60s coffee table.

Scandinavian glassmakers adopted a cooler, more rational approach, creating both studio glass and mass-produced utilitarian ware with equal commitment. Working for Iittala, Finnish designer Timo Sarpaneva won awards both for his glass sculptures and his functional i-line tableware, for which he designed everything from drinking vessels to packaging. Moving on from the smooth free-blown shapes of the '50s, Sarpaneva and his fellow designer Tapio Wirkkala experimented with texture. Glass was blown in wooden molds, creating a barklike surface that became a distinctive feature of '60s table glass. In addition to Iittala and Nuutajärvi in Finland, leading Nordic factories included Kosta and Orrefors in Sweden and Holmegaard in Denmark, where artistic director Per Lütken created handsome organic designs.

While art glass flourished, developments in the manufacture of heat-resistant glass also affected everyday kitchenware. The Schott factory in Germany produced glass casserole dishes and drinking vessels using a new, fully automatic process. Corning in the U.S. introduced colored and decorated Pyrex dishes to attract the housewife, and one of the most coveted appliances in the '50s kitchen was an American-style electric oven, complete with a glass panel (a hugely popular innovation) through which you could keep an eye on your cooking.

"Handicrafts and industrial production go hand in hand. We need human design, sensitivity and the power of machines." Timo Sarpaneva

FAR LEFT The tea set with a removable infuser was originally conceived in 1931 by Bauhaus designer Wilhelm Wagenfeld for the Schott factory in Jena, Germany, pioneers in the development of heat-resistant glass. After World War II, and funded by the Marshall plan, the factory was moved to Mainz in West Germany and fully automated. Wagenfeld's design was reworked by Heinrich Löffelhardt to suit machine-operated presses, which permitted the use of much thinner glass, as seen in this postwar service.

LEFT This Italian vase dates from the '50s. Attributed to Venini, it reflects the Italian taste for glowing colors and extravagant glass techniques.

ABOVE These red-and-white cased-glass Gulvases were designed by Otto Brauer for Holmegaard Glassworks in Denmark in the '60s. They were also manufactured in clear glass *(page 17)*, though cased examples with a white lining tend to command higher prices in today's market place.

MATERIALS

METALWARE

Metal was a favorite postwar medium. In the '50s, designers exploited its linear and organic qualities; in the '60s, it took on a shiny, space-age feel, appearing in every form, from tubular coffeepots to chain-mail mini skirts. At the Festival of Britain in 1951, the Skylon, an aluminum-and-steel sculpture, towering 300 feet above the South Bank in London, heralded a new look in metalware: a spindly graphic line, expressed in the wire fruit baskets, plant holders and magazine racks that filled '50s living rooms.

Stainless steel, initially developed for the armaments industry, was transformed from an industrial material into elegant tableware to rival silver.

American-style chrome appliances became popular in the kitchen, and stainless steel replaced silverware on the most glamorous tabletops. British designer Robert Welch drew on his experience as a silversmith to create a whole range of stainless-steel services in contemporary designs for Old Hall Tableware, produced by J & J Wiggin Ltd, the first British firm to manufacture stainless-steel tableware. Welch won

Design Centre awards for his Campden tableware in 1958 and his Alveston line in 1965. Campden (circa 1956) was a joint design with David Mellor, who produced some of the most influential flatware of the postwar period, ranging from the slender Pride in 1953 (which combined a contemporary look with a traditional Georgian feel) to Thrift in 1965 (an economical setting designed for British prisons and hospitals) and Chinese Black in 1975 (made from strip steel with resin handles, its chunky graphic look became an icon of '70s style).

Still in Europe, inventive modern silver was produced by Italian designer Lino Sabattini and Danish sculptor Henning Koppel, whose curvilinear pitchers for Georg Jensen made metal look like a living substance. "When I see how a branch grows organically out of the trunk of a tree, I am inspired by this," explained Koppel. "I seek to create the same organic unity between the body of a jug and its spout." The firms of Gense in Sweden and Stelton in Denmark exported Scandinavian stainless steel across the world. Among Stelton's most famous products was the Cylinda Line tableware (pages 67 and 99) designed by Arne Jacobsen—a set of gleaming, geometrical cylinders that captured the shiny spirit of the '60s.

In 1954, Danish designer Jens Quistgaard and American entrepreneur Ted Nierenberg founded Dansk Designs to market Scandinavian style in the U.S. "From peasant craft to a sophisticated line … Dansk wooden pieces are up to the minute in design, practical and exquisitely crafted," noted one contemporary critic. Scandinavia also promoted the '60s fashion for wooden-handled cutlery, only ousted from the dining room by the arrival of the dishwasher in the kitchen.

While Scandinavian designers sought to give a modern twist to a traditional material, in the later '60s and '70s there was a craving for a more rustic look. '50s Formica was ripped out in favor of wooden panels and stripped-pine tables, as even urban homeowners opted for farmhouse style. "The kitchen should be the most comforting and comfortable room in the house," advised cookbook writer Elizabeth David, whose London kitchenware shop, opened in 1965, sold the same French wooden bowls, mandolins, and chopping boards that formed part of her own influential *batterie de cuisine*. Terence Conran's *The Kitchen Book* (1977) recommended the purchase of beech salad servers and elm salad bowls. "Imagine a fresh green salad in an orange plastic bowl," he noted with distaste. The interest in country tableware grew, and wooden items imported from peasant cultures across the globe decorated the most stylish metropolitan tables.

OPPOSITE Against a wooden sculpture by Brian Willsher is a wooden-cased clock by George Nelson, one of America's most influential postwar designers. From 1949, Nelson produced a range of designs for the Howard Miller Clock Company.
LEFT This cheeseboard and ice bucket are by Skjøde Knudsen for Skjøde Skjern circa 1960.
BELOW LEFT This ice bucket is by Finn Juhl circa 1958. The salad servers and tray are by Jens Quistgaard for Dansk. Combining industrial techniques with hand-craftsmanship, Quistgaard's wooden tableware was solid, stylish, contemporary, and today is highly collectible.

If one material typified the Scandinavian Modern look in the '50s and early '60s, it was wood, particularly teak. Denmark, in particular, used this wood to produce high-quality, sophisticated furniture and household items, which were exported across the world.

MATERIALS
WOOD

Plastic technology, developed during World War II, revolutionized peacetime products and the look of the contemporary home. Not only was it break-resistant, but it could also be molded into user-friendly shapes.

MATERIALS
PLASTICS

In the '50s kitchen, Formica countertops and vinyl coverings attracted housewives with the promise of bright modern colors and easy-clean surfaces. "Want a miracle floor—a sparkling plastic wonder that glows with beauty and laughs at dirt?" seduced a typical advertisement. Overcoming early difficulties with melting and fading, manufacturers recommended plastic tableware as the perfect product for the rough and tumble of family life.

Melamine, refined in the '40s when the US Navy commissioned unbreakable dishes for maritime use, was a favorite '50s choice. Russel Wright's Residential melamine dinnerware, launched in 1953, combined fluid organic shapes with a choice of fashionable colors, and came with a 10-year guarantee against breakage. A host of manufacturers entered the melamine market, and by 1960, *Good Housekeeping* magazine claimed that one in four American families owned a set of plastic dishes.

In the '60s, plastic moved from the kitchen to the living room, with plastic furniture. Italy, Germany, and Scandinavia were all leading producers of stylish pieces. While manufacturers were eager to stress its elegance, plastic was also the perfect medium for cheap and cheerful products, including many icons of period kitsch. Even at its most practical, an element of fun was often introduced: the success of Tupperware, created by American scientist Earl S. Tupper in 1945, was due as much to the invention of the Tupperware party as it was to the patented airtight seal.

OPPOSITE **This plastic Thermos, creamer, and sugar bowl are by Danish designer Erik Magnussen, who worked for Stelton in the '70s.**
ABOVE **This parmesan dish was designed in 1968 by Enzo Mari for the Italian company Danese. This is a modern reissue, produced for Alessi.**
RIGHT **This Helit German ashtray typifies the bold shapes and bright colors of '60s and '70s plastics.**

ABOVE **One of the reasons for the success of melamine was that it could take strong dyes, as exhibited by this orange-and-white Gaydon service.**

THIS PAGE **The Nature Study service was created by Terence Conran for Midwinter in 1955. The matt-black glaze showed off the curvaceous lines of Midwinter's new Fashion shape and contrasted with white saucers decorated with sketches of leaves and butterflies.**

OPPOSITE ABOVE **Eva Zeisel's expressively organic Town and Country cruets were produced for Red Wing Pottery USA in 1946.**

OPPOSITE BELOW **These black-and-white plates were all designed by Jessie Tait for Midwinter circa 1955–56. The patterns are Monaco** (top)**, Tonga** (right)**, and Zambesi** (left)**. Zambesi was a very popular design and inspired many imitations.**

The crisp definition of black and white was a favorite choice for a young generation setting up home. "Cream was what your parents had," remembers one '50s homeowner. "Black and white was clean, sharp, and modern. It was the New Look."

BLACK AND WHITE

Monochrome designs appeared on everything, from textiles to tableware, and in every style, from figurative to abstract. White saucers decorated with freehand sketches were coordinated with black cups and coffeepots, the all-over color emphasizing the silhouette of the new, organic shapes.

Contemporary designers brought art to the tabletop. Piero Fornasetti's *trompe l'œil* black-and-white plates *(pages 10–11)*, were inspired by both surrealism and historical prints. In contrast, American ceramicist Eva Zeisel drew on the biomorphic forms of contemporary abstract sculptures to produce her Town and Country tableware. Black-and-white textiles, spattered with dots and dashes, mirrored the "drip and splash" canvases of Jackson Pollock.

A spindly black graphic line was a characteristic feature of '50s style, expressing itself three-dimensionally in wirework furniture and decorative objects, as well as on flat surfaces. Ceramics were covered with scratchy, hand-painted black lines, and the '50s saw a craze for zebra-striped tableware, paving the way for the Op-art fashions that were to follow in the '60s. Pioneered by painters including Bridget Riley and Victor Vasarely, Optical Art used geometrical abstraction to disrupt and fragment the vision, creating the illusion of movement. The necessary mechanical precision made it a style ripe for mass production, and, sometimes to the dismay of its fine-art originators, dizzying black-and-white "Op" patterns decorated household items from tablecloths to drinking glasses.

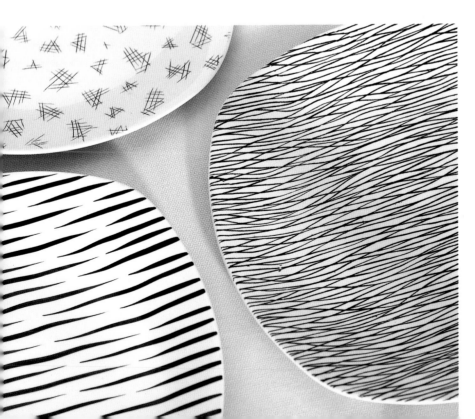

Plastic canisters and melamine tableware came in every conceivable shade, and manufacturers boasted that husbands could choose a Formica tabletop to match their wife's eyes! Even the most functional appliances no longer had to be white. Refrigerators came with colored doors; everything from food-mixers to ice crushers were made in a choice of "gay" colors.

"Mix and match" was a favorite term, with tableware produced in coordinating combinations. Two-tone ceramics became fashionable (one color inside, another outside), as did "harlequin" tea and coffee sets, in which every guest could have a different cup and saucer. "Never before has the hostess had so many colors to choose from," thrilled one '50s woman's journal, and magazines offered helpful advice on how to mix tableware "like paints on a palette," even suggesting dressing to match the dishes.

Once rationing finally came to an end, food and drink, too, became more decorative. The return of the cocktail party brought colorful drinks served in equally bright "domino" cocktail glasses, the theory being that if everybody had a different glass, no matter how much you drank, you would remember which one was yours! "A buffet table should display a colorful array of refreshments ... exciting enough to make 'conversation pieces,'" advised a typical period cookbook, in which every dish was smothered with a multicolored garnish. But if culinary fashions could veer to extremes, tastes in tableware were more sophisticated. Objects came in complementary tones—pastel shades were a '50s favorite—mixed but still matching, and paving the way for the clashing colors of the psychedelic '60s.

COLORS
MULTICOLORED

LEFT These teacups in blue, green, pink, and yellow reflect the '50s fashion for mix-and-match tableware.
BELOW Hornsea slipware vases in mauve, green, and yellow demonstrate the trend for delicate, pastel colors in the home.
RIGHT Two-tone tableware (one color inside, another out) was a period favorite, both in ceramics and other media. These bowls, made from steel with bright enamel interiors, are Danish Krenit ware. They were designed in 1953 by Herbert Krenchel and manufactured by Torben Oskov

After the drabness of war, there was a huge lust for color in the home. Plastics, in particular, helped transform the kitchen from a sterile white zone into—according to the advertisements—a colorful, wipe-clean playground.

NATURALS AND NEUTRALS

The rampant artifice of many '50s products, with their use of plastics, metal, and acid colors, was countered by a more naturalistic approach. Scandinavia, in particular, while pioneering some of the most experimental design of the period, also remained firmly committed to a culture of traditional craftsmanship and native materials. Landscape was a major source of inspiration, offering strong textures and colors that were earthy and neutral.

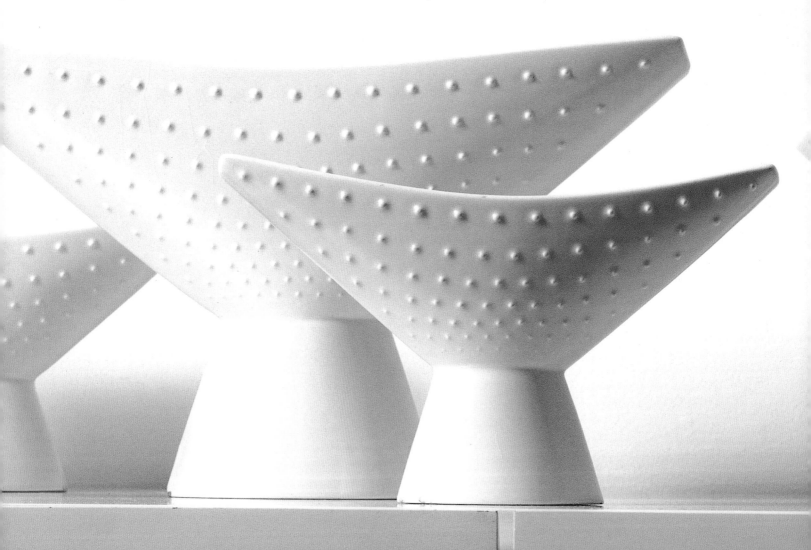

"We feel that nature is the true source of lasting beauty," explained Finnish designer Kaj Franck, "does anyone ever tire of looking at a graceful birch … or a beautiful sunset?" Glass reflecting snow and ice, wooden tableware, hand-thrown pots, and handwoven, natural textiles all became part of the Scandinavian Modern look, adopted around the world.

As changing eating habits were reflected in tableware, the '60s interest in health food and vegetarianism was matched by a desire for equally natural and healthy-looking receptacles.

The Craftsmen Potters Association, London's most fashionable shop for handmade ceramics, was opened in the same street and by the same person as the capital's most trendy vegetarian café, "Cranks"—its name deliberately parodying the health-food fad. Small potteries, such as Rye and Troika, flourished, and even big commercial companies sought to give mass-produced dishes a handmade, earthenware feel. If the '60s palette was psychedelic, it was also brown, cream, and oatmeal, the colors of granola.

MAIN IMAGE **The Home Décor line of vases was designed by John Clappison for Hornsea Pottery in 1960.**
INSET **The Poole Twintone coffee service dates from the '50s. The mottled gray "seagull" glaze was matched with a number of solid colors, here brown. Neutral in color and contemporary in shape, Twintone was a very successful line.**

COLORS

TECHNICOLOR

If '50s colors were harmoniously mixed and matched, in the '60s, every color of the rainbow could be blended together.

THIS PAGE **Even the most functional kitchenware was sprinkled with psychedelic flowers. The shaker and rolling pin are from the Gaytime line by Lord Nelson Pottery, UK; the casserole is by Figgjo Tableware in Norway; and the floral canisters are from Staffordshire Potteries.**

Influenced by Pop art, designers favored bright tones and a hard-edged graphic style. Classic motifs include the target, the Union Jack, and blow-up numbers and letters—images stripped of their traditional significance and applied to domestic items in glorious technicolor. Red, white, and blue was a favorite '60s combination and a symbol of Carnaby Style. If "Swinging London" was the center of Pop and Mod fashion, then "Dreaming California" (notably, San Francisco), was the birthplace of psychedelia, inspired by hallucinogenic drugs, spread by the hippie movement, and expressing itself in every form, from music to posters to tableware. Whitefriars glass Bark vases *(page 89)*, launched in 1967, the year of the summer of love, came in a choice of technicolor hues, including Kingfisher Blue, Tangerine and Lilac. Orange, purple, and pink were popular decorative shades, appearing on the most mundane objects, from storage canisters to rolling pins. In Britain, Morphy Richards manufactured an orange toaster decorated with shocking-pink Mary Quant daisies. Marimekko, Finland's leading textile firm, produced glowing furnishing and dress fabrics in Op-art patterns offering total immersion in multicolored spots and stripes.

OPPOSITE **The target was a major Pop-art emblem. American artist Jasper Johns became famous for his target paintings in the '50s, and by the following decade, the target motif was seen on everything from T-shirts to album covers. This plate was designed and produced by British designer Paul Clark in 1965, and shows how Pop symbols even filtered through to '60s tableware.**

RIGHT Curving vessels by Poole Pottery UK, who experimented with contemporary freeform designs in the '50s.

FAR RIGHT ABOVE This white bowl with a turquoise interior is by Mitzi Cunliffe, who created a series of sculptural, asymmetric shapes for Pilkington Pottery in Britain in the early '50s.

FAR RIGHT BELOW Dishes from the Century line designed in 1957 for Hall China USA by Eva Zeisel, a pioneer of organic modernism in tableware.

ORGANIC

After the severity of '30s modernism and wartime austerity, there was a desire for soft, swelling feminine forms. The kidney-shaped coffee table was a '50s favorite, and similar rounded designs appeared in every medium. The popularity of this amebalike form has been attributed to new scientific discoveries (microscopic views of molecules), to camouflage patterns, and to the influence of modern painting.

Tableware was stripped of dirt-catching angles and decorations. Innovations included the rimless plate, its soft-cornered shape poised between square and circle, providing a perfect surface for all-over decoration and

bringing an end to the English habit of putting salt on the edge. Pitchers and teapots swelled like pregnant women. Curves replaced straight lines and asymmetry was a distinctive feature. The Poole coffee set *(page 33)* literally reflects the waisted, hourglass shape, its base flowing out like a circle skirt.

Centers of organic design included Scandinavia, where nature was a major creative influence, and the United States, home of new technology and manmade materials. Though inspired by nature, organic shapes did not necessitate organic materials—plastic was perfect for biomorphic forms.

THIS PAGE A keynote of organic design, with its undulating, freeform shapes, is a balance between art and nature. These white vases, by Swedish designers Stig Lindberg and Gunnar Nylund, suggest both abstract sculpture and the shapes of shells or seed pods. Working for Gustavsberg, Lindberg was inspired by nature both in terms of form and decoration, and in the '50s created a line of painted vessels based on leaf designs.

Fashion and furnishing often go hand in hand. If the classic '50s silhouette was the hourglass, epitomized by Christian Dior's "New Look," design in the home was equally curvilinear.

SHAPES
GEOMETRIC

If the '50s were curvaceous, the '60s were streamlined. This look was perhaps most famously embodied by Twiggy, leading model of the day and teenage icon of swinging London, with her waiflike boyish figure, short haircut, and long, mini-skirted legs.

As in fashion, tastes in tableware veered to the tall, slim, and tubular. The can-shaped coffeepot, pioneered by British designer Susie Cooper in the '50s, became a favorite feature on the '60s table. The simple cylinder provided a perfect medium for all manner of decorations. Portmeirion, which adopted the can shape in 1962, decorated sets with everything from the Greek key motif to Victorian prints *(page 104)*. Its slender coffeepots towered some 14 inches high. "I had to stand up to pour out the coffee," remembers one '60s housewife.

Everywhere, '50s organic flowing forms were replaced by straight-sided vessels and simple geometric shapes—oval and quartic plates gave way to circles, and the cone was a popular shape for cruet sets. Flush lids also enhanced the clean geometric lines; this feature contributed to the look of Arne Jacobsen's Cylinda Line stainless-steel tableware *(pages 67 and 89)*, which—from pots to packaging—was entirely based around the cylinder. Designers experimented with the geometric look throughout different media. In flatware, there was a fashion for thick, short-pronged forks, asymetric knives, large, shallow-bowled spoons, and salad servers terminating in flat disks. Carafes with elongated necks and geometric-shaped vases were a feature of contemporary glassware, their abstracted forms complemented by jubilantly psychedelic colors.

OPPOSITE **This Hornsea set is typical of its time both in its shape and the use of flat lids. Removing the knop not only simplified the silhouette of pitchers and canisters, but also made them cheaper to produce, easier to stack, and harder to damage.**
ABOVE **These German porcelain demitasses show that cups, too, followed the tall, cylindrical look.**
ABOVE LEFT **This ceramic bottle vase is by Guido Gambone, one of Italy's leading postwar potters.**

THIS PAGE **A porcelain set created by German designer Nick Roericht in 1959 and manufactured in the U.S. by Thomas China and Crystal from 1961. Space-saving tableware was much in demand, and this stackable dinnerware, designed when Roericht was still a student, was widely admired and much imitated.**

"Espresso coffee was to the '50s what marijuana was to the '60s, the drug of choice for a generation," remembers Terence Conran. The '50s saw the rise of coffee drinking, and coffee bars became favorite teenage hangouts, with Formica tables, juke boxes, and gleaming chrome espresso machines. Coffee once again was easily obtainable, resulting in a huge variety of grinders, pots, and percolators.

Thanks to increased prosperity and the introduction of extended credit, sales of electrical equipment boomed. Kitchens were increasingly filled with labor-saving appliances: refrigerators, food mixers, toasters. These machines, with glamorous curves and bold automotive styling, gave way by the end of the '50s to more minimal, rational shapes inspired by German design. Space was at a premium in the smaller homes and apartments built in the postwar period, hence the development of stackable dinner sets, built-in kitchens, and sleeker appliances. Bernadotte & Bjørn's 1950 nesting Margrethe bowls were among the earliest melamine items produced in Scandinavia, and are still in production today. Easy to store, hard to break, and light to lift, these stylish, heat-resistant bowls came in different colors and were a perfect addition to the contemporary kitchen.

New technology in the living room also affected eating habits. With the introduction of the television set, families abandoned the dining table in favor of snacking in front of the box. Ceramic manufacturers responded by introducing a combined cup and plate, marketed as a "telly set." Television not only created demand for instant food; it advertised it, too. Swanson's came up with the first TV dinner in 1953. Vesta curries and paellas—"just add water"—first appeared on British supermarket shelves in 1961, and, "ready in only 20 minutes," introduced many to their first taste of exotic foreign food.

Cheaper travel and the growth of the package vacation in the '60s stimulated interest in the cuisine of other countries, as did the surge in foreign restaurants. Avocado dishes and fondue sets became new additions to the middle-class wedding list. Fashionable '60s kitchen equipment included French Le Creuset casseroles, Greek olive-wood salad bowls, and tall glass jars for Italian spaghetti, reflecting the diversity and increasingly global nature of home cooking.

New forms in tableware reflected fashions in food as increased prosperity brought greater choice to the table.

SHAPES

NEW FORMS FOR NEW FUNCTIONS

TOP **Bernadotte and Bjørn's nesting Margrethe bowls proved that plastic could be a serious rival to more traditional materials. The designers examined many vessels before coming up with their final ergonomic form, which included an integral handle and spout and a rubber ring to stop the bowl from slipping.**
ABOVE **In the '20s and '30s, combined cups and plates were known as "breakfast" or "tennis" sets. In the '50s, they were relaunched as "telly sets;" this example is by Denby Potteries.**

PATTERNS
ABSTRACT

Abstract patterns flourished on postwar tableware, reflecting contemporary art, modern scientific imagery and the new shapes of the space age.

Abstraction entered the home through interior designers. "People who would never have hung an abstract painting on their walls, hung the boldest abstract curtains on their windows. It was a very exciting time," remembers British designer Lucienne Day, who created some of the most important textiles of the '50s. Day's influences included painters such as Joan Miró and Paul Klee, and contemporary art affected every medium. Scandinavian glass echoed the sculptural forms produced by Constantin Brancusi and Henry Moore. Ceramic tableware was decorated with geometric shapes and abstract expressionist doodles.

'50s abstract patterns are often characterized by fluid, organic forms and a sinuous, hand-drawn line. In the '60s, this linear delicacy gave way to bigger, bolder shapes and a more rigid geometry. Barbara Brown's Focus pattern *(page 108)* is a carefully controlled design of squares and circles, favorite motifs

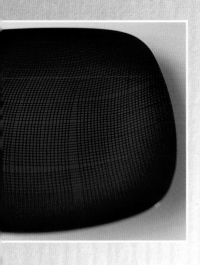

These dinner plates are all by Midwinter. The Chequers pattern (below) was produced by Terence Conran first as a textile, then in 1957 as a tableware design. The freehand pattern with its uneven lines and sketchy motifs reflects the humane approach to abstraction characteristic of '50s style. A similarly random effect also appears in the designs created by Jessie Tait (opposite): Mosaic (top right) and Homespun (bottom), created in the early '60s, and Magic Moments (top left) from the '50s. INSET '60s abstraction in art translated well to tableware, as proved in this Op-art dish.

of the period. Abstraction became increasingly slick and mechanical through the '60s, with Pop-art motifs and Op-art patterns.

If modern art was one major influence on abstract design, another was contemporary science. From the discovery of DNA to the detonation of the H-bomb, this was the "atomic age." The world of hidden shapes revealed in the microscope was a huge source of inspiration. The Festival Pattern Group's imagery, based on crystal structures, for the Festival of Britain (1951) stimulated a fashion for molecular designs.

Science affected shape as well as pattern. George Nelson's 1949 Ball wall clock, a starburst form of metal rods and wooden spheres, was based on 3D models of atomic structure. This "line and blob" look (also known as the cocktail-cherry style) filtered throughout '50s design, from black wirework fruit baskets standing on colorful ball feet to the mighty Atomium, central building of the 1958 Brussels Expo, a model of an iron molecule 360 feet high. Space exploration took designers higher still, with shiny plastic, stainless steel, and strong geometric shapes filling the home.

FIGURATIVE AND FLORAL

The '50s fashion for decoration resulted in a wealth of figurative designs celebrating modern life. Ceramics illustrated with pictures of fresh food marked the end of wartime shortages. Contemporary furnishing was another favorite subject: images of leggy plant stands and boomerang tables appeared on dinner plates. And with the return of European travel, manufacturers reflected the desire for Continental glamour with Riviera scenes and pictures of chic Parisian ladies.

The British manufacturer Midwinter sent artist Hugh Casson to the South of France in 1953/4; his festive watercolors of ports and cafés resulted in the bestselling Cannes (shown here) and Riviera ceramics.

A new age needed a new decorative vocabulary. The animals that expressed the '50s were the French poodle and the long-necked cat, appearing in every form, from teacups to tablecloths. Rejecting traditional florals, designers examined flowers with the analytical eye of a scientist. Terence Conran drew on his juvenile experience as a lepidopterist to produce the ceramic pattern Nature Study *(page 28)* in 1954, reducing plants and insects to black-and-white skeletal structures. In Jessie Tait's Flower Mist, the naïve,

almost abstracted, blooms are again pared down to the minimum.

The '60s saw a more "Pop" approach to nature. Perhaps the most famous flower of the decade was Mary Quant's daisy, which not only appeared on fashion products, but sprung up throughout the decorative arts. As the hippie revolution shook the world, flower power blossomed, and the slick, graphic daisy gave way to swirling tendrils and fantastical blooms.

The '50s and '60s saw the rise of the teenager, and as young people gained more spending power, manufacturers catered to their interests. Tableware was decorated with rock-and-roll images, and Beatles fans could drink from Fab Four glasses and eat from Beatles plates. In an age of protest and slogans, typography also became an important decorative form. Mugs were featured blow-up numbers and letters, and fashionable companies, such as tinware manufacture Dodo Designs and Portmeirion Pottery, revived Victorian imagery with a Carnaby Street twist *(pages 104–7)*.

OPPOSITE '50s Midwinter plates demonstrate the fashion in floral and botanical decoration. Terence Conran's 1955 Salad Ware (below left) shows colorful sketches of vegetables, providing a celebratory record of changing eating habits. Plant Life (top left), again by Conran, circa 1956, reflects the period craze for indoor pot plants. While prewar ceramics are often decorated with springtime forms and colors, '50s tastes were more autumnal. Falling Leaves (top right) was designed by Jessie Tait in 1955, and Flower Mist (bottom right) was produced by Tait in 1956.
LEFT Susie Cooper, who had remained in the vanguard of ceramic trends since the '20s, produced the Carnaby Daisy coffee set in 1968, clearly inspired by Mary Quant's logo and the swinging London scene.
ABOVE Springtime china was manufactured by Hornsea in the '60s and provides a variation on the favorite daisy motif.

LIVING WITH RETRO TABLEWARE

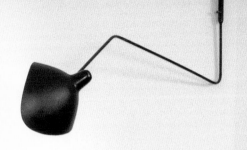

THE POSTWAR LOOK

With the end of World War II came a pressing need,
particularly in battle-weary Europe, for new housing, and
an equally powerful desire for a new style of furnishing.
Technologies developed during the war revolutionized the
peacetime interior. Steel, plywood, and plastic were used
to meet the demand for more flexible, space-saving, and
affordable household objects. A young generation of architects
and designers, inspired by abstract art and scientific progress,
transformed the postwar home with New Look design.

LEFT **Some of the best in European and American design can be seen here. The shelving system by French designers Jean Prouvé and Charlotte Perriand offers the perfect means to display eclectic pieces of the time. On the top shelf are vases by Jean Cocteau, and the white '50s wavy-rimmed planter on the shelf beneath is by Poole. The freeform bowl below that is by American-born sculptor Mitzi Cunliffe, who designed a line of thick-walled, asymmetric, and sculptural ceramics for Pilkington Tile and Pottery Company in the early '50s.**
RIGHT **Slatted benches, which could serve either as tables or seating, were a popular feature of the period. This Tokyo bench, designed by Charlotte Perriand, displays large pottery vases in bright contrasting tones created by French ceramicist Georges Jouve.**

Clear and colorful, this interior conjures up the new "contemporary" look of the early '50s with its combination of bold organic shapes and fine graphic lines. The postwar fashion for open-plan rooms and more flexible living arrangements was reflected in modern furnishing—lightness and mobility were a key feature.

In 1944, American architect George Nelson (pioneer of the indoor shopping mall) came up with the concept of "storagewall," a series of multipurpose, mix-and-match storage units that sounded the deathknell for the traditional sideboard. Combining display shelves and cupboards (often multicolored like an abstract painting), these versatile systems were produced by everyone from leading international designers to mass manufacturers. The structure could either be placed free-standing, serving as a room divider between living and dining areas, or set against the wall, as shown here. The lines of the unit contrast with the organic shapes displayed on it. The two vases on the top shelf are by Jean Cocteau. Inspired by Picasso, he began after the war

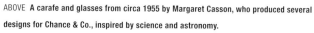

ABOVE A carafe and glasses from circa 1955 by Margaret Casson, who produced several designs for Chance & Co., inspired by science and astronomy.

RIGHT This dining table is by U.S. sculptor-designer Isamu Noguchi, who produced a range of wire-and-formica tables for Knoll, circa 1955. It is set with a '50s linen tablemat by Robert Stewart and stainless-steel tableware designed by Robert Welch, whose sculptural Oriana flatware was produced by Mappin and Webb in 1957.

FAR RIGHT A mug designed by Norman Makinson for Wedgwood to commemorate the Festival of Britain in 1951.

to experiment with ceramics. "Pottery provides me with more possibilities and satisfaction than painting, drawing, or writing," claimed the writer and artist in 1959. "I'd give a good many well-known pictures for a beautiful pot."

Much as ladies of the period, in their huge, bell-shaped skirts, wobbled perilously on their sharp stiletto heels, so, with chairs; the generous, organic curves of seat and back were supported on slender metal legs, their New Look silhouette reflecting wartime technology and the development of new materials. Laid out on Isamu Noguchi's table with its twisted wire base, Robert Welch's curving, abstracted metalware contrasts with Robert Stewart's linen, whose sketchy illustration is a typical example of period whimsy.

If chairs and tables almost seemed to float in space on their spindly supports, then space itself was an important influence on decorative pattern. Glassware and ceramics were adorned with astronomical imagery as well as futuristic buildings such as the Skylon and the Dome of Discovery—built for the 1951 Festival of Britain—which captured the optimistic mood of the moment and heralded the dawning of the space age.

Whereas the lines of the furniture are long, lean, and architectural, the ceramics are curvaceous, capturing period taste for organic, asymmetric, and sculptural forms, for which clay was a perfect medium.

ABOVE FAR LEFT The large Peanut vase sitting on Robin Day's 1954 Interplan sideboard and the platter in the foreground were designed by Alfred Burgess Read for Poole Pottery. Employed by Poole in the '50s, Read introduced freeform, organic shapes and replaced traditional florals with delicate abstract patterns in subtle colors. The white bowls, created by Robin Platt and Cairn Young for Rosenthal, are inspired by '50s design.

ABOVE CENTER '50s Rosenthal orchid vases designed by Fritz Heidenreich and a Macassar ebony lamp, designed by Alexandre Noll in 1959, stand on a sideboard by British architects John and Sylvia Reid.

ABOVE Under a 1955 lamp by Georges Jouve is Rosenthal's Service 2000, designed in 1954 by Raymond Loewy and Richard Latham. Echoing the New Look hourglass shape, it was one of Rosenthal's most popular lines.

This English home shows '50s styling at its most elegant. Set against chairs by designers Terence Conran and Robin Day, and a coffee table by sculptor Eduardo Paolozzi, this international array of tableware shows the latest in chic entertaining. The age of austerity has come to an end, and the scene is set for a postwar party.

The seating in this living room dates from the '50s and is by Robin Day, Britain's leading furniture designer of the period. The textile on the wall was designed circa 1954 by Marian Mahler for David Whitehead. The table, dating from around 1956, is inset with tiles by British sculptor Eduardo Paolozzi. It is set with modern glassware, a '50s Scandinavian enameled metalware dish, and from the same period, a Midwinter bowl.

NEW ENTERTAINING

Often heralded as the father of American cooking, James Beard's 1940 title *Hors d'Oeuvres and Canapés* was the first major cookbook devoted exclusively to cocktail food. And the party was just beginning. By 1959, Beard was serving up flambés, crêpes, and daubes to his *House & Garden* readership.

In the postwar period, eating habits became more informal and the choice of what to eat more exotic. Cookbook writer Constance Spry opened her first book in 1956 with a chapter on cocktail parties—and everybody wanted to entertain. "Buffet suppers and cheese and wine parties became all the rage," remembers Marguerite Patten, one of Britain's first TV chefs, "and the most important thing was that everything should look as decorative as possible."

Manufacturers of tableware latched onto this desire for fun and frivolity. Midwinter, one of Britain's most pioneering ceramics firms, launched their Stylecraft line in 1953, followed by the Fashion line in 1954. "You may 'fashion style' your table with the latest tableware, just as you would buy the latest style in dress design," claimed director Roy Midwinter. A number of Midwinter pieces are shown in this interior, including the 1956 pattern Plant Life, designed by Terence Conran and decorated with indoor pot plants, which—like elaborate flower arrangements—became a popular decorative craze in the '50s home. Period advertisements showed Plant Life plates covered with

"We have also fallen in love with food again," wrote Terence Conran, noting that the process of marketing, cooking, and choosing different equipment and tableware "is again one of the great pleasures of life."

THIS PAGE The height of dinner-party chic: a Le Creuset fondue set and a Danish teak-handled dish serves up this "exotic" cuisine. Stainless-steel tableware became popular during the '50s and '60s. The 1956 Plant Life plates are designed by Terence Conran for Midwinter, as is the Salad Ware sifter from 1955.
OPPOSITE These Midwinter plates and bowl are from the Oakley line, designed by Jessie Tait. The metal-legged chair was designed in the '50s by Terence Conran.

croissants, tapping into a growing interest in European food. Similarly, on the opposite side of the Atlantic, the Kennedys had employed a French chef. And, within three months of its publication in 1961, the first book by Julia Child on French cooking had sold 20,000 copies.

American women were discovering entertaining as an art form, and home cooking became increasingly adventurous. The flambés, soufflés, and cream-laden cakes of the '50s gave way in the '60s to daubes, cassoulets, and peasant-style cooking, rather than Cordon Bleu cuisine. The fondue was another favorite dinner party choice. Like the newly available foods and wines, tableware was imported from across the globe. Le Creuset's (established 1925) colorful French cast-iron casseroles became extremely fashionable in the '60s.

This interior includes German porcelain, Italian glassware, and Danish metalware, reflecting both the international nature of contemporary styling and the huge wealth of objects available to the postwar homeowner. "When did you last hear the word austerity?" demanded *Queen* magazine in 1959, announcing the arrival of "an age of unparalleled lavish living.... It is the age of BOOM."

LEFT Laid out on a 1954 Robert Heritage sideboard, ready for a buffet dinner, are plates and a cruet set from Rosenthal's 1976 Suomi line, designed for the German factory by Timo Sarpaneva. Alongside are two Hornsea vases and a '50s space-influenced lamp produced by the Dutch company Philips.

FAR LEFT AND BELOW A '50s butterfly chair and floor lamp (again by Philips) set the scene. The modern glassware on the left of the cabinet is by Italian designer Ettore Sottsass, and the carafe is by Margaret Casson. On the table is a variety of '50s bowls: a two-tone Melaware dish, a Krenit-ware bowl, and a small Midwinter dish from the 1958 Patio line.

COCKTAIL HOUR

Popular in the '20s and '30s, and impossible during the war, cocktail parties returned to fashion in the '50s, when at last people were free to entertain again.

The postwar passion for cocktails stimulated a wealth of decorative household items. In the '50s, the home bar became an object of desire, with styles ranging from discreet rectilinear cocktail cabinets to elaborate novelty designs such as the boat bar, simulating the prow of the ship and coming complete with portholes and gilt-metal anchor.

Cocktail glasses were produced in multicolored domino sets and decorated with everything from abstract patterns to bathing beauties. Pin-up girls (a term that emerged during World War II when servicemen pinned up girlie pictures in their barracks) were a favorite decorative motif on cocktail ephemera; other popular themes included gambling (playing cards and dice, for example) and animals, particularly poodles and cats.

In this interior, however, kitsch extravagances are rejected in favor of a more sophisticated and intimate cocktail twist. The long '50s tubular Raye lampshade by French ceramicist Roger Capron hangs over a handsome Danish ice bucket, the thick-walled glass mirroring its frozen contents. Postwar glass designers took much of their inspiration from ice and snow. In 1969, Whitefriars

THIS PAGE **The ultimate accessories for a sophisticated retro cocktail party are here: tall, elegant amber glassware; a '60s Norwegian enamel plate decorated with an Op-art pattern; the '70s Eiger decanter and drinking glasses from Whitefriars; '50s Krenit-ware enamel bowls with yellow interiors; and a Midwinter Patio pattern plate designed by Jessie Tait circa 1958.**
OPPOSITE **A tall ceramic Raye pattern lampshade designed by french ceramicist Roger Capron.**

The perfect cocktail requires the classic cocktail glass— the stem should be long enough to protect the conical bowl from the heat of the hand, its opening wide enough to display a decoration or garnish.

launched its Glacier line of glass tableware, inspired by Scandinavian designers and reflecting the '60s fashion for textured glass. Similar in style, the Eiger drinking glasses and decanter were designed by Geoffrey Baxter for Whitefriars in the early '70s, the icy ridged surface created in a wax mold.

Vintage objects from the '50s, '60s, and '70s combine seamlessly with contemporary pieces in this apartment, creating a cocktail of tableware. The shapes of the modern drinking glasses and, in particular, the chromium cocktail shaker, hark back to the Art Deco period. It was in '20s America—the jazz age—that the cocktail really came into its own, stimulated by prohibition and the fact that illegal, and often unpalatable, liquor tasted better when mixed with other ingredients. After repealing prohibition in the early '30s, Franklin Roosevelt mixed the first legal martini in the White House, and Nikita Khrushchev went so far as to call this powerful drink "America's lethal weapon." The martini captured the inspiration of designers as well as drinkers, its glass becoming a recognized symbol of sophistication in the '50s and '60s—to be hung in neon outside cocktail bars around the world.

OPPOSITE **A vintage soda siphon with silver mesh and modern cocktail glasses sit on a red enamel tray made by Emalox in Norway.**
ABOVE **A Danish glass ice bucket with a wicker handle.**
ABOVE RIGHT **The Cylinda Line stainless-steel ice bucket, tray, and corkscrew were designed in the mid-1960s by Arne Jacobsen for Stelton, Copenhagen. The cocktail shaker and pitcher are modern, but the period influences are clear.**

NORTHERN LANDSCAPES

Light and airy, this interior reflects
the Scandinavian Modern look that
became the height of international
fashion in the '50s and '60s.

"More beautiful things for everyday use" was the motto of the Scandinavian designers who rose to international prominence after the war. Climate was crucial to the development of the Scandinavian Modern style. Harsh weather conditions emphasized the importance of a warm, comfortable home, and ordinary household objects were required to be both practical and attractive. "The Scandinavian has a word for it, 'brukskunst' (useful art)," explained critic Eileene Harrison Beer. "He believes that food for his body should be served on tableware handsome enough to be food for his soul."

Culturally and geographically isolated, particularly during the war years, Scandinavian designers drew on their own heritage and surroundings. The Nordic landscape itself was a major inspiration. Organic shapes, native materials, and colors and textures reflecting earth, plants, and ice are all classic features of Scandinavian design, combined with clean contemporary lines.

Pioneer of this humane Modernism was the Finnish architect Alvar Aalto. Commissioned to build the Paimio tuberculosis sanatorium in 1929, he rejected the metal furniture considered hygienic for such institutions, because "psychophysically these materials are not good for the human being. Wood," he declared, "was better for the human touch." Using cantilever techniques more usually applied to metal, Aalto developed a new line of mass-produced plywood furniture, such as the tea trolley *(overleaf)*, which established processed wood as a perfect material for the modern age. The curvilinear biomorphic forms used by Aalto, both in furniture and other media such as glassware, became part of Scandinavian vocabulary in the postwar period.

While designers experimented with technology in their quest for economical mass production, nature

OPPOSITE **Large picture windows were a feature of '50s architecture, making the external landscape part of the internal decoration. This ideal is reflected in the organic shapes, colors, and materials of the decorative ware on the window sill** (from left to right)**: a tall contemporary vase by Jonathan Adler; a small vase by Carl Harry Stålhane for Rörstrand; a wooden bowl by Dansk International Design; and a wooden bowl by Artiform, Italy.** ABOVE AND RIGHT **Glass from Holmegaard, Denmark, and striped ceramic bowls by Stig Lindberg for Gustavsberg, Sweden. The modern teapot is by Ö Design, Sweden.**

RIGHT AND BELOW The white vases poised elegantly on George Nelson's '50s cabinet are by the modern American ceramicist Jonathan Adler. The ovoid vase resting on an Alvar Aalto table is by French designer Jean Besnard, and the stoneware bowl is by Carl Harry Stålhane for Rörstrand. Stålhane trained as an artist, and many of his designs in the '50s were inspired by abstract painting and sculpture. Charles Eames's 1946 molded plywood folding screen complements the natural colors and organic forms.

Scandinavian designers pioneered everyday tableware and furnishings that were handsome, affordable, and practical. Combined, as they are here, with classic works by leading American and European 20th-century designers, these pieces, with their neutral colors and clean lines, create a look that is calm, elegant, and humanely modern.

ABOVE The cane-handled porcelain teapot was designed by Ulla Procopé in 1957 for Arabia. The plate is by Stig Lindberg for Gustavsberg, decorated with the leaf patterns with which he experimented in the '40s and '50s.

LEFT The Model No. 901 tea trolley by Alvar Aalto dates from 1935/36. The plates and salad servers are by Dansk International Design. Jens Quistgaard's teak VIII-8 ice bucket, also produced by Dansk, was designed in 1960 and is a masterpiece of streamlined modernism, and a perfect cocktail accessory for the contemporary living room.

"People work better, feel better, and are happier when they have everyday objects of beautiful colors and shapes around them in their homes," observed Swedish social reformer Ellen Key, "regardless of how modest these objects may be."

OPPOSITE The ceramics on the dining table are by Rörstrand (established in 1726). In the postwar period, the company became known both for handcrafted studio pottery and for colorful contemporary tableware, such as the Redtop line, from which the casserole and bowl are shown here.
RIGHT The chair is by Charles Eames, reflecting his revolutionary experiments with molded plywood in the '40s. The elongated wooden tray is by Dansk International Design.

and tradition remained important touchstones. In the '50s, Stig Lindberg created a line of colorful ceramics for Gustavsberg, many inspired by leaf patterns. Gustavsberg was typical of Scandinavian factories in that it produced commercial tableware and handmade studio pottery, combining the industry of the present with the artistry of the past. "Handicrafts and industrial production go hand in hand," advised Finnish designer Tapio Wirkkala. This policy was practiced at Arabia in Finland and Rörstrand in Sweden, where brightly colored oven-to-table ware (a '50s favorite) was manufactured alongside craft pieces. Holmegaard, under the designer Per Lütken, dominated the Danish glass scene after World War II, producing both series ware and experimental pieces in contemporary shapes and colors.

If there was one material more than any other that really summed up Scandinavian style, it was wood, particularly teak. Dansk International Design (established in 1954) exported Scandinavian-style wooden tableware and accessories across the world. Produced by Danish designer Jens Quistgaard in 1960, the VIII-8 ice bucket showed how solid teak could be sculpted into the most elegant modern shapes. It was this combination of contemporary lines with traditional materials that made Scandinavian design such an international success. "It was very fashionable, but it wasn't scary," remembers one homeowner who furnished her apartment in the early '60s with Danish furniture and Swedish tableware. "It was comfortable, practical, and a pleasure to live with."

Half a century on, the '50s ideal of a dream American kitchen is still very much with us. This modern example mixes old, new, and retro-inspired pieces to create a kitchen where appliances are not something to be hidden away, but objects to be celebrated in all their shiny, functional glory.

MODERN KITCHEN

After World War II, with the demobilization of their menfolk and the disappearance of servants for all but the most wealthy, women abandoned their wartime jobs and moved into the kitchen. "This is the room which more than any other you love to keep shining and bright," enthused a '50s *Woman's Own* magazine. "A woman's place? Yes it is! For it is the heart and center of the meaning of home. The place where, day after day, you make with your hands the gifts of love." And not just with the hands, but preferably with the help of new "labor-saving" appliances that became the ultimate objects of feminine desire in the '50s.

Period advertisements show women in party dresses, frilly hostess aprons and high spike heels grinning with delight as they point to their state-of-the-art stoves or washing-machines. "—and it's so much *fun* besides!" boasts a 1951 advert in *The American* for an automatic pop-up toaster. And in a typical promotion, American Kitchens promised that its modern built-in units would save housewives "1,000 steps a day." Perhaps more than any other room in the house, the kitchen was most affected by the postwar consumer boom.

The '50s also saw the introduction of the built-in kitchen and, thanks to the "Magic of Plastic" (Formica surfaces, vinyl flooring), bright "gay" colors replaced the prewar hygienic whites and creams. The U.S. pioneered the powerful concept of the dream kitchen filled with modern machines "to help you streamline

OPPOSITE **The mid-century kitchen combined shiny new appliances with bright colors, modern materials, and new shapes. All these things are reflected in this contemporary kitchen in** (clockwise from top left) **the modern plastic bowls; the retro-inspired Model XI Coffee Machine designed in 1995 by Luca Trazzi for the Spanish manufacturer Francis Francis; the classic Poole eggcups; and the '70s Coffee Grinder by Krups.**
ABOVE **A Master of Life Juicer and retro-patterned glasses with matching chopping board.**

Though American in styling, this Dualit 4-slice toaster was conceived by British engineer Max Gort-Barten, who founded his company in the '40s. Its good looks blend perfectly with the shiny appliances of the modern kitchen.

your housework." In creating mixers, blenders, juicers, and other appliances, manufacturers used shiny chrome, bright enamels, and bold, curvaceous shapes inspired by space rockets and automotive styling. In addition to striving to make it more efficient, American industrial designers turned the kitchen into a glamorous place, and their effect can still be felt in the modern kitchen seen here, which mixes new and vintage to gleaming effect.

Contemporary objects such as the Master of Life juicer and Waring's Professional Blender clearly reflect the exuberance of American retro styling. Waring first began producing professional blenders for American soda fountains in the '30s, and with its geometrical lines, this blender shows an Art Deco influence that persisted in electrical goods in the '40s and '50s.

The electric toaster was invented by British firm Crompton and Co. in 1893, and the first pop-up toaster was produced in the U.S. in 1919. The Dualit toaster, seen here, created circa 1946 by British engineer Max Gort-Barten, was also inspired by American prototypes

and, still in production today, is now regarded as a design classic. Features include a "stay-warm mechanical ejector" and though originally designed for commercial use, it is now a popular household model.

Germany also paved the way in home-product design. The '70s coffee grinder in this kitchen is by German manufacturer Krups (established in 1846), which, although famed for its rational approach, still could not resist the attraction of color which today, as Luca Trazzi's modern blue coffee machine shows, we take for granted in the kitchen.

In creating refrigerators with "fashion-colored doors," and salmon-pink food mixers, '50s designers proved that white goods did not necessarily have to be white. They also showed that the kitchen could be not only a functional place, but also a fun and stylish one. 50 years on, equipped with modern and vintage items from around the world, the modern kitchen can still embody the same ideal.

Prohibition enhanced the attraction of the American soda fountain which, from the 1880s until the 1960s, was very much the social center of small-town life, particularly for teenagers. Thanks to film and TV, its appeal extended across the Atlantic. This selection of soda-fountain ice-cream glasses combined with a chromium bar stool reflects the enduring fascination of retro Americana. The Waring Professional Blender was also a classic American-made product.

If '50s kitchens were all shiny chrome and colorful Formica, the '60s and '70s saw a return to a more natural look. With its wooden furnishings and handcrafted earthenware pots, this interior has all the components of a traditional farmhouse kitchen, combined with a truly modern awareness of style and space.

While '50s housewives reveled in the pleasures of plastic surfaces, processed food, and labor-saving appliances, the '60s and '70s brought different aspirations. "A possible reaction to a cold and clinical kitchen, new pleasures are to be found in baking bread, brewing beer and growing vegetables," observed Terence Conran's *The Kitchen Book* (1977). "People yearn to return to a self-sufficient life, but most want kitchens that combine efficient modern equipment with the old-fashioned virtues of a warm atmosphere and comfortable surroundings."

Two of the figures responsible for inspiring this change were Julia Child and Elizabeth David. Elizabeth David was the most influential British cookbook writer of the postwar period. From her first volume, *Mediterranean Cooking* (1950), David's books promoted not just traditional peasant dishes from France, but also traditional country cooking equipment: rustic clay pots, cast-iron casseroles, copper pans, and wooden utensils—many originating from France.

Likewise, Julia Child's 1961 book *Mastering the Art of French Cooking* threatened the reign of TV dinners, meatloaf, and corned-beef hash. In 1963 she took her talents to the small screen with *The French Chef*, extolling the virtues of copper pans to a yet wider audience of women.

The crafts movement flourished in Britain after the war, particularly during the '60s, when shops such as the Craftsmen Potters Association in London became popular with a middle-class clientele in search of the good life and an honest pot. This table is covered with stoneware pots and storage jars produced by a number of different potters, all still active in Britain (from left to right): a John Leach bread pot; bowls by Richard Batterham; Svend Bayer's lidded storage jar; a casserole by Andrew and Joanna Young; a bread pot by Richard Batterham; and a loop-handled pitcher by John Leach.

HOMESPUN WARES

OPPOSITE **Even industrial ceramics of the '70s aped a handmade feel. Beneath the shelves of glass storage jars stand three canisters from Hornsea's Heirloom line, designed in 1967, their colors typical of the period. The white pottery jar is by Colin Haxby. BELOW** (from top left) **Two pottery storage jars by Rörstrand; two enamel containers; a Stephen Price jug; a salt-glazed cheese strainer. The bowls below are by Richard Batterham, and the terracotta beanpot is French.**

At a period when functional implements were hidden in Formica cabinets, in the kitchen/dining rooms of Elizabeth David and Julia Child these everyday items were kept on open display, on pine hutches or hanging from the walls as in a general store. The look was subsequently adopted by fashionable '60s retailers (Williams-Sonoma in San Francisco, and Habitat and Elizabeth David's own shop in London), and slowly filtered into the family kitchen. Chuck Williams, founder of Williams-Sonoma, wrote of the '60s, "Julia Child's cooking show was finding an audience. She would show how to make a soufflé one night, and the next day people would come in asking about soufflé dishes."

Through the use of natural materials, earth colors, and traditional items, this kitchen harks back to an idealized rural past, while the uncluttered surfaces and sculptural forms show a keen awareness of modern design. Objects are arranged both so that they are practical and close at hand and to show off their individual forms. Colors are warm and harmonious, and the combination of wood, glass, pottery, and metalware provides a variety of textures. "The perfect kitchen," wrote Elizabeth David, "would be really more like a painter's studio furnished with cooking equipment." And, some 25 years later, one feels she would have approved of the present interior.

THIS PAGE On the tabletop, the cast-iron candlestick is by British designer David Mellor, as is the coffeepot from the 1969 Au Pair line, in stainless steel with a colored acetal resin knob and handle.

OPPOSITE On the coffee table is another coffeepot, again by Mellor, from the Pride line—made from silver with leather-covered handles.

"The craftsman who designs for mass production …
should create an object of sculptural worth with good proportions,"
Jens Quistgaard

"Earthenware casseroles ... should be in every household," advised Elizabeth David, adding that cassoulets and daubes would lose "flavor and a good deal of their charm if cooked in an ordinary saucepan."

Set off by white blinds and walls, this corner is devoted to blue. The chair is by British designer Robin Day. On the table stands a decahedral kingfisher-blue Banjo vase made by Whitefriars Glass circa 1969 and designed by Geoffrey Baxter. Next to it is a blue glass Gulvase bottle by Holmegaard, dating from the '60s, a Scandinavian covered jar, and a clear blue Continental glass bowl and drinking glass.

Pale walls and stripped floors prove a fitting backdrop for a collection of brilliantly colored, boldly shaped and richly textured decorative objects, reflecting the inventiveness of postwar design. By grouping objects according to color, separate areas of interest are created in each room.

COLOR PARTY

The cult of youth that directed music and fashion in the '60s also had its influence in the home, as the rainbow colors of contemporary clothing spread to the applied arts.

The decahedral blue glass Banjo vase on the living-room table in this apartment and the orange vases shown on the sideboard *(overleaf)* are by Whitefriars Glass. This new "textured" line was designed by Geoffrey Baxter in 1966 and launched in 1967, the year of the Summer of Love, when color became psychedelic. Vases were blown into textured molds—the mold for the cylindrical Bark vases was actually lined with tree bark, forming an irregular, lumpy surface. The Banjo vase represents the more unusual, abstracted shapes that were also produced. All this glassware came in a variety of glowing colors—kingfisher blue and tangerine were added to the line in 1969, closely followed by meadow green and eggplant.

Next to the Banjo vase is a blue bottle vase by Holmegaard, one of Denmark's most inventive postwar glass factories. These bottles—or Gulvases—were designed by Otto Brauer from 1962.

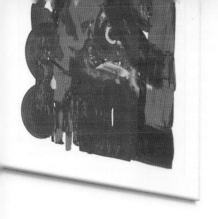

THIS PAGE On the glass table is a selection of vintage continental glassware and ceramics, red in color and extravagant in form. On the sideboard are white textured vases from Hornsea Pottery's Home Décor line, designed by John Clappison from 1959 to 1962. Clappison's works are becoming increasingly sought by collectors today. The armchair and ottoman are by Hans Wegner, one of Denmark's leading furniture designers in the '50s.

OPPOSITE LEFT The mustard-colored lamp stand is by Royal Doulton and stands alongside a selection of vintage American ice-cream cups.

OPPOSITE RIGHT A cylindrical Bark vase and two other tangerine vases from the Whitefriars textured line. Produced 1969–74, tangerine was an extremely popular color.

They were produced in various sizes and came in a range of colors, and were made in both clear and cased glass. Their extruded, elongated shape was a feature of '60s design.

The collection of red vases is also typical of the period in the use of extravagant form, inspired by sources ranging from abstract sculpture to 19th-century pharmacy bottles to psychedelic posters. Designers prided themselves on their individuality. "We make no traditional products," John Clappison, design director of Hornsea Pottery proudly informed *House & Garden* magazine in December 1968. The ceramics shown here illustrate this variety in Hornsea's products: the white vases on the sideboard reflect period interest in textured decoration, while with the candy-striped Rainbow planters and the Springtime cruet set, the accent is firmly on color and pattern.

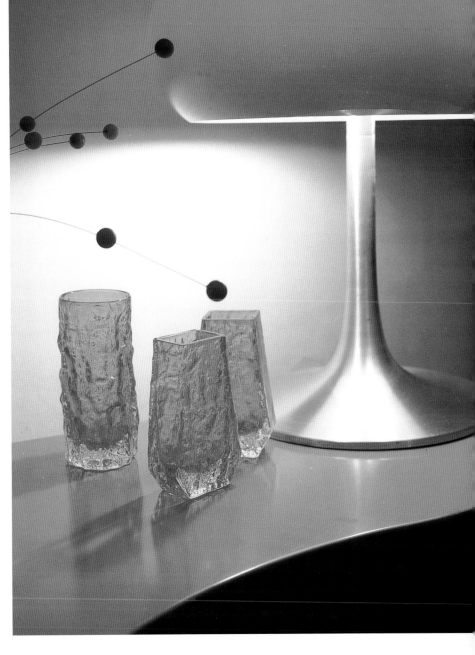

"The Beatles really pricked the old fuddy-duddy balloon and the ripples touched and reshaped every aspect of our domestic lives," ceramic designer David Queensberry told HOUSE & GARDEN magazine in 1968.

THIS PAGE The gray vases on the sideboard are by Hornsea Pottery, the slipware pattern reflecting the factory's interest in producing textured ceramics. Also by Hornsea are the Summit mustard pot, with its striped ribbed pattern, and the Springtime cruet set, in which three-dimensional decoration has been replaced by flat surface design. The dinner plates are by the Meakin factory, in the Studio shape which, designed in 1964, served as a base for a huge range of '60s patterns. The plate, far left, is by Midwinter in the bestselling 1966 Spanish Garden pattern, recalling the patterns of Islamic tiles and inspired by a Liberty print tie.

THIS PAGE The planters and
vase are from Hornsea Pottery's
Rainbow line, introduced in
1961. Their pattern reflects the
period desire for more colorful
ceramics and a strong interest
in textured decoration.

Laid out in a modern kitchen, this Scandinavian tableware was produced in the '50s. Created for everyday use, half a century on these objects still fulfill their function perfectly, showing the enduring nature of good design.

SCANDINAVIAN UTILITY

If '50s America gave birth to the concept of the "Dream Kitchen," filled with big, bold, and colorful items, then a very different kitchen was dreamed up in postwar Scandinavia. "I would like to design things that are so obvious that one hardly notices them," claimed Finnish designer Kaj Franck, whose everyday tableware created what one '50s newspaper

described as a "revolution on the dining table." Set on the table seen on this page are dishes from the Kilta line, Franck's most famous design, produced for Arabia in 1952. What made this set revolutionary was its simplicity and versatility. The clean, geometric shapes were stackable and multi-functional, and pieces could be used in the oven. Kilta came in a choice

OPPOSITE The dishes laid out on the table are from the Kilta line designed for Arabia by Kaj Franck in 1952, and the waisted green carafe was produced by Nuutajärvi in 1954, again designed by Kaj Franck. Both the glass pitchers and Kilta (now called Teema) remain in production today. The flatware is by Arne Jacobsen, and the one-piece plastic chairs were designed in the '60s by Verner Panton. THIS PAGE The melamine Margrethe bowls in the foreground were designed in 1950 by Sigvard Bernadotte and Acton Bjørn. The bowls and pans behind are Danish Krenit ware, made from steel with bright enamel interiors; this colorful kitchenware has become highly collectable.

of different colors, and customers were encouraged to mix and match rather than having to buy a full set at a time of national shortages. The undecorated earthenware was cheap to produce, affordable in price—and of course it looked good.

Franck applied the same principles to his utilitarian glassware. The waisted carafe he designed for Nuutajärvi Glassworks in 1954 came in several colors. The elegant shape, echoing the hourglass fashions of the day, resulted from his attempt to find a form that would avoid the expensive process of manufacturing a handle and was slender enough to be held in one hand.

It is this stylish rationalism that lies at the very heart of Scandinavian design and that has made Nordic tableware so successful and so long lasting. Still in production today, the melamine Margrethe bowls by the kitchen sink *(page 93)*, were designed by Bernadotte and Bjørn in 1950. The team analyzed bowls from across the world in order to come up with this attractive, nesting design, which was strong, heat resistant and ergonomically shaped.

But Scandinavian design was not just about practical styling. This is, after all, the part of the world that gave us the plastic troll, favorite toy craze of the '60s. Designers met the '60s, in all its exuberance, head-on. Marimekko—founded by Armi and Viljo Ratia in Helsinki in 1951—became internationally famous for its boldly patterned, technicolor textiles, which, in addition to being used for furnishing the home, were worn by every dedicated follower of fashion, right up to the First Lady Jacqueline Kennedy. Combining the modestly rational with the flamboyantly decorative, this sleek interior encompasses this rich variety of Scandinavian style.

"Whatever it is, the Danes sell it, the Swedes manufacture it, the Norwegians ship it, and the Finns design it."
Scandinavian saying

ABOVE **The Polygon coffee set above was created by Finnish designer Tapio Wirkkala for Rosenthal in 1973. Next to it stands a stainless-steel Au Pair coffeepot, produced in 1969 by David Mellor, who, like many British designers of his generation, was profoundly influenced by Scandinavian tableware.**
RIGHT **A collection of '60s Gulvase bottle vases from the Holmegaard glass factory in Denmark.**
OPPOSITE **The textile in the background was designed in the '60s for Marimekko by Maija Isola. The ceramics on the table are by the Swedish Gustavsberg factory, and the steel and cane chair is by Danish designer Poul Kjaerholm.**

With its white walls, boldly geometric plastic furniture, and shining stainless-steel tableware, this modern interior reflects the space-age look of the '60s. The conquest of the moon was the greatest technological event of the decade, and the visual vocabulary of space travel filtered down to earth, affecting everything from fashion to furnishing.

SPACE-AGE STYLE

THIS PAGE **Space-age colors and shapes are illustrated in a Danish teak-handled plastic ice bucket made in the '60s, and modern Finnish cups, by Arabia, set against Verner Panton's '60s stacking chair.**

OPPOSITE **Anna Castelli Ferrieri's Round-Up storage system, created for Kartell in 1969, supports a plastic thermos, creamer, and sugar bowl designed by Erik Magnussen for Stelton.**

On October 4, 1957, the Soviet satellite Sputnik 1 orbited the earth in 96 minutes, stimulating a host of satellite-inspired items, from preserve pots to cigarette boxes. The U.S.S.R. had won the first stage of the space race, but it was the U.S. that put a man on the moon, and on July 20, 1969, an estimated 60 million people worldwide tuned in to watch the Apollo landing. Designers, too, caught space fever. A symbol of '60s optimism and undoubtedly the most glamorous expression of the Cold War, the space race had a huge effect on contemporary design, inspiring new technology and imagery.

In fashion, couturiers such as André Courrèges and Pierre Cardin sent models down the Paris catwalks in silver sequin trousers, white plastic boots, and visored helmets. "Courrèges invents the Moon Girl" enthused *Vogue* in 1964. As this apartment demonstrates, interior designers took up the baton, creating suitable furnishings for moon girls and boys in their vinyl and metal clothing. As in fashion, white and silver were favorite colors. Andy Warhol lined the Factory in New York with silver; and London's most swinging boutiques, such as Just Looking on the King's Road, covered their walls with polished aluminum. A cheaper alternative was to paper a room in your house with silver foil. "It looked very "'with-it,' and it was fantastic for making your pot plants grow!" remembers one London journalist.

If metal was one fashionable material, another was plastic, perfect for space-age furniture. Italy designed some of the most inventive plastic seating of the decade, ranging from the blow-up chair to the vinyl-covered bean bag, both symbols of a new throwaway society. The Milanese firm Kartell (established in 1949) invested heavily in plastic technology. Designed by Anna Castelli Ferrieri in 1969, the Tondi or Round-Up

White and silver were the ultimate space-age colors, and plastic and metal the favorite shiny materials. Combined with strong geometric and abstract shapes, even everyday tableware took on a space-age look.

German company Nagel's '50s
metal candleholders can be
built into different patterns,
mirroring atomic shapes and
structures. Equally futuristic is
Arne Jacobsen's stainless-steel
Cylinda Line tableware,

designed for Stelton in 1967.
These strong geometric shapes
sit perfectly against the
abstract-inspired furnishings—
Eero Aarnio's Pastilli rocking
chairs and La Chaise (designed
by Charles and Ray Eames).

As "square" became a postwar term denoting old-fashioned, so rounded shapes emerged as a '60s favorite. Furnishings and tableware lost their straight edges in favor of globe forms that looked like astronaut's helmets.

storage system is one of the first series of furniture to be produced in injection-molded ABS plastic. The system came in modular units that could be stacked together as storage cabinets or used separately as stools and tables, meeting a contemporary desire for flexible, more informal furnishing. Its cylindrical shape was a period favorite, reflected in the Thermos set designed by Erik Magnussen for the Danish company Stelton in 1977. Produced first in stainless steel (later in plastic), and including a lid that opens and closes automatically when the Thermos is tilted, this practical and stylish design was Stelton's bestselling product.

Scandinavia further pioneered the development of plastic furniture and household objects. Verner Panton's stacking chair (designed in 1960, but not manufactured until 1967) was one of the first, successful single-piece chairs. Coming in a choice of bright, fashionable colors, its flowing form was rendered possible only through new advances in plastic technology. Finnish designer Eero Aarnio also used synthetics to create dramatic, modern forms. His 1967/68 fiberglass Pastilli chair was intended for both indoor and outdoor use, and provided a space-age interpretation of the rocking chair. But it was in the field of household technology (lighting, radios, record players, televisions) that space-age forms really took off like a rocket. One of the most iconic designs of the period was the circular television, reflecting the shape of an astronaut's helmet. Inspired by the Apollo moon project, British designer Arthur Bracegirdle produced the first globe TV set for Keracolor in 1969. The oval Aphelion TV set in this apartment was designed by Stephen Foster in the early '70s. Combined with this bold furniture is a selection of shiny stainless-steel tableware, including Arne Jacobsen's 1967 Cylinda Line coffee set and Sergio Asti's 1976 Boca flatware. Whereas in the '50s stainless steel was brushed to give it a more muted appearance, in the '60s and '70s the look was polished and shimmering.

Popularized by cult TV series and films such as *Barbarella* and Stanley Kubrick's *2001*, space-age design is today extremely collectible—conjuring up the glamour of the '60s and providing a decorative symbol of that "giant leap for mankind" when science fiction was turned into space fact.

LEFT **This blue glass Provence bowl, dating from the '50s, was created by Danish designer Per Lütken for Holmegaard.** RIGHT AND BELOW **Resting on a modern plate, this stainless-steel Boca (Italian for "mouth") flatware was produced for Lauffer in 1976 by Italian architect Sergio Asti. The cruet set is from Arne Jacobsen's 1967 Cylinda Line service for Stelton. The Aphelion TV set was designed in the early '70s by Stephen Foster.**

HIPPIE HOME

With its swinging furniture and technicolor tableware, this interior is decorated in '60s psychedelic style. Flower power may have begun as an antimaterialistic movement, but its colorful imagery quickly spread from the hippie pads of Haight-Ashbury to chain stores across the world.

"Gradually the with-it world of fashion has been extending its influence," observed *Ideal Home* magazine in 1966. "Not content with deciding the clothes we wear, fashions now have a strong say in the homes we live in as a result furnishing has become more fun—more lively and lighthearted." A major youth fashion of the day was psychedelic style. Psychedelia emerged in the mid-'60s—most notably from San Francisco, capital of flower power and the hippie movement. Inspired by hallucinogenic drugs ("Turn on, tune in, and drop out," urged LSD guru Dr. Timothy Leary), psychedelia affected everything from music to clothing and, as this apartment shows, filtered into the home. Textiles were perhaps the most successful psychedelic household products. You didn't have to take LSD to enjoy a vision of "tangerine trees and marmalade skies"—all you needed to do was close the curtains!

For a young generation moving into studios and student apartments, mobility was all important. Posters replaced pictures, and a salient feature of the

OPPOSITE **Hanging basket chairs were produced in many European countries and could be bought very cheaply. On the mirrored table is a '60s plastic ice bucket. The candleholder, designed by Graham Bishop, is decorated with a target motif, a favorite Pop-art symbol; and the placemat is covered with a swirling psychedelic pattern.**
THIS PAGE **This glass bowl is attributed to Whitefriars, which produced a variety of colored pieces in the '60s.**

LEFT These cups and canister are from the Totem line designed in 1963 by Susan Williams-Ellis for Portmeirion Pottery. Produced in various colors (white is most sought by collectors today), Totem was the company's bestselling design in the '60s.
FAR LEFT BELOW This Comfortable Corsets coffeepot and sugar bowl are also by Susan Williams-Ellis for Portmeirion. This is part of a group of ceramics launched in 1965 decorated with 19th-century prints and advertisements.
FAR LEFT ABOVE Tangerine was a popular '60s shade, as seen in these period pieces: an orange faience coffee set from Denmark; a floral cushion; and a tin tray by Dodo Designs showing Britannia seen through psychedelic eyes.
BELOW A set of bowls in the Madeira pattern designed by Nicholas Jenkins for Midwinter in 1965. Decorated with Art Nouveau revival flowers, the fabric is Prince of Quince, designed by Julia Glynn-Smith for Conran Textiles.

hippie pad was the rejection of traditional matching living-room furniture in favor of multicolored floor cushions. Cane furniture was another choice. Popular designs included the exotic Peacock chair and the hanging basket chair seen in this apartment *(page 102)*—the ultimate swinging seat, which was suspended from the ceiling or from its own metal frame, was endlessly featured in magazines.

Color and pattern were also crucial elements. The kaleidoscopic tones and swirling designs featured on psychedelic posters and record covers appeared on the most humble domestic items, from placemats to cookie jars. Orange, pink, and purple were favorite shades, and designers drew on a wide range of imagery. Portmeirion was one of the most inventive British potteries of the day. Resting on the furry rug are ceramics from the Totem line, its raised pattern inspired by both primitive symbolism and Victorian tiles. Portmeirion also produced the Comfortable Corsets line, decorated with prints from a Victorian underwear catalog. Nothing was sacred, and every image was ripe for reinterpretation. Dodo Designs, a fashionable British company specializing in Pop household products, produced a line of tinware covered with traditional patriotic images in day-glo tones.

The late '60s saw a host of decorative revivals: Victorian, Art Nouveau and Art Deco; but in addition to looking to the past, designers also drew influences from abroad, particularly Asia, favorite destination on the hippie trail. Illustrated among the group of tins on this page is a selection of black, pink, and blue canisters in a Moorish-inspired pattern called Salome and produced by Ian Logan for JRM Designs in 1967. The diversity of these tins is typical of the period, and perhaps the keynote of psychedelic design is its cheerful and colorful ecleticism. One of the most successful designers of the period was Peter Max, who produced the Happy tray and also features on the front cover of *Life* magazine (September 5, 1969). "His art is a savory rehash of Art Nouveau, Op, and Pop," noted the magazine. "Max hopes his designs will bring happiness and harmony into millions of people's lives." At the age of 29, the New York artist was already earning $2 million a year from his psychedelic patterns, which appeared on everything from clocks to napkins, epitomizing the mass commercialization of a once-alternative style.

"Alphonse Mucha, Max Ernst, René Magritte … Dulac, contemporary comic books, ancient book illuminations—all boiled down to make a visionary and hallucinatory bouillabaisse," noted the OBSERVER in 1967. "The whole world can be plundered for decoration," agreed Richard Neville, founder of Oz magazine. "Copyright is ignored."

RETRO LOUNGING

In this postwar apartment, vintage tableware is used to reinforce a subtly retro look, bringing together elements from different decades and echoing shapes and colors of retro furnishing and decor.

This apartment is inspired by '60s and '70s style. Brown and beige were favorite colors in '70s interior decoration, ranging from the coffee-and-cream Art Deco revival look to the earthy tones and nubbly textures that reflected more rustic tastes. The continuing popularity of open-plan homes stimulated demand for modular seating, such as this sofa system that can be pushed into corners and adapted to the shape of the room.

"Because today's floor plans tend to be very open, traditional approaches to furniture arrangement no longer necessarily work," advised *House & Garden's Complete Guide to Interior Decoration* in 1970. "Sofas, chairs, and accompanying tables often form islands of relaxation, subtly connected so that they can be enlarged, reduced or merged on occasion. Contemporary upholstered pieces are so low, they barely interrupt the sweep of space around them." This low-slung furniture—combined with developments in polyurethane foam—meant that designers could produce both enlarged and varied seating shapes for the home.

The pictures in this apartment recall '60s Pop art, and both their geometric patterns and the overall color scheme of the space are picked up by the tableware. The '60s Focus coffee pot is manufactured by the British company Midwinter. Moving away from Midwinter's freeform shapes of the '50s, David Queensberry had introduced the straight-sided cylindrical Fine shape in 1962, inspired by the form of a milk churn and capturing the geometrical

LEFT **Barbara Brown's Focus pattern—originally conceived as a textile—was translated into ceramics, as seen on this coffeepot produced by Midwinter in 1964. The '60s design illustrated here in the bold, geometric pattern and form of the coffeepot is in stark contrast to the soothing organic curves of other ceramics in the apartment which belong to later decades.**
RIGHT **Modular seating systems were a popular feature of open-plan living arrangements. The candelabra on the table is by Platt and Young for Rosenthal.**

Circles, disks, and target patterns became the height of decorative fashion in the '60s, appearing in Op- and Pop-art paintings, in contemporary clothes and jewelry and on everyday household objects.

mood of the moment. Designer Barbara Brown had already produced a series of textiles for the London home-furnishing store Heal's when, in 1964, she created Focus, her first work for Midwinter. Inspired by Op art, the gray, brown, and black pattern of circles and squares proved a bestseller.

Op, Pop, and Mod fashions affected tableware as well as clothing. In 1969, Burgess and Leigh launched their Orbit pattern. "Fresh and scintillating as if from outer space!" boasted the advertisement. "This thrilling new idea in modern tableware is a bold exercise in spatial relationships." Orbit came in two trendy color variations: green and blue, and orange and red.

Small wonder that after the extravagant and jubilantly psychedelic color schemes of the '60s, in the '70s there was a move toward more muted, natural tones. For example, Timo Sarpaneva's Suomi set designed for Rosenthal in 1974, and shown on the dining table *(pages 112–13)*, relies not on color for its effect, but on sculptural shape, its compact organic forms inspired by the round, smooth pebbles on Finland's coast. While in the '60s designers embraced space-age technology and looked to the stars, in the '70s they came back down to earth again. The backlash against the exuberance and optimism of '50s and '60s Modernism began, and fashion moved toward the more traditional and conservative. Muted tones took over, with glassware in tobacco-smoke grays or glowing amber shades, and ceramics in soothing browns.

Hornsea pottery enjoyed considerable success in the late '60s and '70s with their brown ceramics, ranging from the country-kitchen-style Heirloom pattern *(page 82)* to the more sophisticated lines of the Contrast tableware, introduced by Martin Hunt in

Circles within circles and spheres cut into cubes were typical of '60s pattern and form, and these shapes continued to fascinate designers into the '70s. OPPOSITE Orbit plates by Burgess and Leigh drew on Op-art imagery, while the modern dip tray beside them recalls sculptural designs that were popular in the '60s and '70s. LEFT The modern bowl beside the bed again recalls the period interest in geometrical shapes. In contrast is the black Denby Pottery freeform bowl below. BELOW This elegant amber glassware—made popular in the '70s—includes contemporary stemware by Bowles and Linares.

ABOVE **This '70s smoked-glass carafe and drinking glasses set was made in Denmark. Smoked glass was a popular medium, both for tableware and in furnishings, with glass-topped tables a common feature in the '70s home.**

1975. In this apartment is a tea set in Hornsea's Lancaster pattern from the Contrast line, partially glazed in dark chocolate brown, black, and white. The solid and chunky design is typical of the decade that gave birth to the platform shoe. The long slender cylinders of '60s tableware—which we see in Midwinter's Focus coffeepot—were replaced by shorter, squatter forms with thick curvaceous handles. Flatware, too, changed shape in the '70s, as influential metalware designers like David Mellor produced large, flamboyant shapes with broad shafts and boldly graphic blades, bowls, and prongs.

Set in the brutalist architecture of a famous postwar apartment building (planned in 1959 and completed in 1972), this home is filled with vintage tableware that both enhances the decorative mood of each room and reflects the changing fashions of the '60s and '70s.

LEFT This Suomi coffee set was designed by Timo Sarpaneva for Rosenthal in 1974 and manufactured from 1976. Its sculptural forms are made from porcelain and stainless steel. The vintage stainless-steel candlesticks are by Stelton, Copenhagen.

ABOVE This Lancaster tea set, from the Contrast line, was designed by Martin Hunt for Hornsea Pottery Company in England from circa 1975.

ITALIAN INSPIRATIONS

Modern glamour is the key note of this Italian-inspired apartment, which combines strong architectural shapes with luxurious, sensuous materials. The elegantly monochrome color scheme is interspersed with bursts of bright color provided by Italian glass and metalware. The Italian design ethos of complementing art with industry was the formula for creating a look that was supremely beautiful, yet perfectly functional. Here, hard and shining surfaces contrast with wood, leather, and fur to create a variety of textures that are stimulating to the eye and comfortable for the body—the essence of LA DOLCE VITA.

Understated yet elegant modern furnishings—such as this modular seating designed by Antonio Citterio for B&B Italia in 1997—provide a fitting backdrop to show off retro tableware. On the coffee table is the Bombé coffee set designed by Carlo Alessi in 1945. The stainless-steel ashtrays in the foreground were created by Achille Castiglioni for Alessi in 1970. The plexiglass-and-chrome lamps were designed by Massimo Vignelli in 1965 and manufactured by Arteluce.

"In Italy," claimed Gio Ponti, "God made the plains, mountains, lakes, rivers, and sky; but the profiles of the cathedrals, facades, churches, and towers were shaped by architects. In Venice, God created only the water and the sky. The remainder was made by architects." Perhaps only an Italian designer could put God and architects on a level footing, but this statement certainly indicates the importance attributed to design and architecture during the reconstruction period in Italy. The country had been devastated by World War II, and there was an immediate need for housing and household goods. Manufacturers exploited new materials and commissioned architects to produce everything from furniture to electrical appliances.

Architects and industrial designers received identical training in Italy, resulting in a close relationship between applied and industrial arts. The Espresso coffee machine, invented by Achille Gaggia in 1946, and the Vespa motor scooter, produced by Paggio in 1945, are perhaps the two most potent examples of this new aesthetic. Widely exported, these gleaming state-of-the-art objects symbolized not just Italian style, but the emergence of the teenage revolution, inextricably associated with coffee bars and scooters. Promoted by films such as Fellini's *La Dolce Vita* (1960), the Italian look became extremely fashionable, not

LEFT **These tall Oxford chairs were created by Danish architect Arne Jacobsen for St. Catherine's College, Oxford. Completed in 1963, the college was Jacobsen's favorite project. The chairs, with their elongated backs, were originally designed for "high table" in the college dining room. These later versions have been upholstered in white leather.**
RIGHT **These colorful Murano glass vases were produced for Neo-Murin by master glassblower Malvino Pavanello.**

RIGHT **This tray was designed by Piero Fornasetti. After studying at the Brera Academy of Fine Arts in Milan, Fornasetti joined forces with Gio Ponti in the '40s. Ponti designed furniture; Fornasetti covered it with two-dimensional images to create a 3D effect. The surrealistic *trompe l'œil* style was to become his trademark for the next 40 years. Ceramics, magazine racks, textiles, even whole interiors were covered with black-and-white prints drawn from historical and contemporary sources. No object was too mundane to receive the distinctive Fornasetti treatment.**

just with Vespa-riding youths in their sharp Italian suits, but with style-conscious homeowners. *Domus* magazine, founded by Gio Ponti in 1928, provided an important vehicle for disseminating the work of new designers, while the Milan Triennale exhibitions helped to establish the city as the international capital of modern design.

By the early '60s, Italy had emerged as the world's leading exporter of modern furniture and furnishing, and this interior is filled with examples of Italian postwar design. Much of the metalware is by Alessi. Established in 1928, the company moved away from craft toward industrial design in the postwar period, experimenting with stainless steel and commissioning a number of celebrated architects and designers to work on its products. The ashtrays and cruet set created by Achille Castiglioni are typical Alessi artefacts: ingeniously practical (the ashtray has an internal spring to keep your cigarette from falling), blatantly shiny, and self-consciously stylish. Lighting was another area in which the Italians excelled. The lamps in this apartment were

created by Massimo Vignelli for Arteluce in 1965, an enlarged and boldly simple design in plexiglass and chrome. Like many Italian architects, Vignelli worked across different media, designing everything from glassware to furniture to packaging.

While modern industrial design was an important aspect of La Linea Italiana, studio-based craftsmanship also flourished, particularly in Murano, traditional center of Italian glassmaking. Designers combined age-old techniques with modern shapes and brilliant colors to create glass of astonishing energy and imagination.

"For an object to be only useful is not enough, each object should have a kind of poetry," claimed the Italian graphic designer Piero Fornasetti, whose eclectic and fantastical prints, extremely popular in the '50s and '60s, decorated everything from tin trays to trash cans.

"Design is a global creative discipline with a strictly artistic and poetic matrix, and not simply one of the many tools at the service of marketing and technology to insure improved production methods and better sales," agreed Alberto Alessi. Perhaps what gave postwar Italian design its seductive appeal was this attempt to meet domestic practical needs not just with new technology and materials, but with an unembarrassed sense of artistry.

"I think that the success of so-called Italian design is due to the fact that design, in my opinion, is not a discipline, but an attitude growing out of one's humanistic, technological, economic, and political beliefs."
Achille Castiglioni

ABOVE **Italian designers embraced the new materials of stainless steel and plastic. The wire Citrus fruit basket designed by Ettore Alessi was produced from 1952, while the 9090 stainless-steel coffeepot designed by Richard Sapper was launched by Alessi in 1979. The modern cup and saucer were designed by Achille Castiglioni, also for Alessi. The '60s pyrex-and-plastic carafe and the plastic juicer by Thermozeta are also Italian.**

LEFT This carafe and matching glasses are by French silver and tableware company Christofle and combine plated metal with Venini glass.

BELOW On this coffee table is an Italian clear and blue glass vase dating from the '50s, and a Murano cased-glass ashtray.

OPPOSITE BELOW RIGHT These cruets for oil and vinegar with counterweighted lids were designed by Achille Castiglioni for Alessi in 1980.

COLLECTING
RETRO TABLEWARE

Shopping for vintage objects is almost invariably more exciting than a trip to a modern department store. When you visit antique strores and flea markets, you never know exactly what you are going to find. You might go with the intention of buying a set of Russel Wright plates and come home with a '60s Scandinavian glass vase because you saw it, you liked it, the price was right, and if you didn't buy it now, you might never see it again.

THIS PAGE **Finnish designer Timo Sarpaneva pioneered techniques in the creation of textured glass, as shown in the ice-like surface of this vase.** OPPOSITE **The glass carafe with a cane grip in place of the more conventional handle was designed by Kaj Franck circa 1955 for Nuutajärvi. The hourglass-shaped vase behind was created circa 1958 by Heinrich Löffelhardt for WMF.**

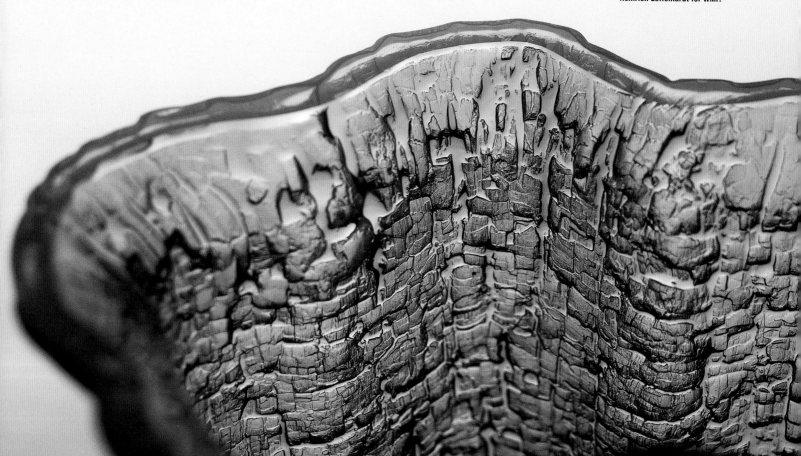

The collectibles shopper has to be prepared to be flexible and, occasionally, courageous—but without being rash. The more you find out about your chosen field, the better you will buy, both in terms of quality and price. There is no substitute for handling objects. An increasing number of dealers and sale rooms are now focusing on modern design, and looking costs nothing except time. Auction previews provide an ideal opportunity for hands-on learning—you are allowed to pick things up, turn them over, and examine them in detail. Dealers are often happy to chat about their particular passion, and even if you're not buying, you can pick up a lot of information, visually and verbally, from simply wandering around antique fairs and galleries. And hopefully you will have fun, which is what collecting is all about.

Growing interest in modern design has stimulated a large number of books and catalogs, and pictorial guides are a useful source of reference. Many subjects have also acquired their own collectors' clubs, which provide an opportunity both to learn more and to meet fellow enthusiasts. The internet is a useful source for contacts and for comparing prices internationally. A growing number of sales now take place on the worldwide web, although before buying from a photograph and a description alone, it is important to know your subject—and to read the full terms of sale.

When buying a vintage item, examine it closely. Condition is crucial to value, and just as important if you are going to be using the object on your own table. Always ask for a receipt that gives the name and address of the seller and a full description of the item, including date and price. Prices will vary depending on current market trends—what's hot and what's not—and where you buy. The same object might well cost more from a specialized metropolitan dealer than from a rural flea market, but what you are paying for is not just their taxes and business costs, but the security and choice of stock that you would expect from an expert. But equally, much can still be discovered in second-hand stores and yard sales. Objects often turn up piecemeal. Though you might not find a complete set of vintage plates or glasses, you can adopt period principles by mixing and matching different items, which makes for an interesting dinner table.

While fragile, rare, or costly pieces might be kept principally for display, the majority of items featured in this book were designed for everyday use and are still being used today. Some additional precautions must be taken. Handpainted china and wooden-handled flatware were not created for the dishwasher, and one of the sacrifices you have to make for style is a bit of old-fashioned dishwashing. But treat objects with due care and attention, and they should last to decorate the tabletops of future generations of collectors.

One of the joys of collecting retro tableware is the sheer pleasure of hunting it down. There is plenty still available, and bargains can still be found. While many people continue to use the china, glass, and metalware that they originally purchased in the '50s, '60s, and '70s, others are throwing it away.

WHERE TO BUY

Key: t = telephone, f = fax, m = mobile

ANTIQUES

Guéridon Gallery
359 Lafayette Street
New York, NY 10012
www.gueridon.com

Ruby Beets Antiques
Poxybogue Road
Bridgehampton, NY 11932
516-537-2802
Painted furniture, old white china, and
kitchenware.

Tickled Pink Antiques
Internet sales only
888-OLD-STUF
www.tias.com
A fine seledtion of silver, porcelain,
pottery, metalware, glass, china, and
dinnerware.

Tri-State Antique Center
47 West Pike
Canonsburg, PA 15317
724-745-9116
www.tristateantiques.com
Specializes in Heywood-Wakefield,
Mid-Century Modern furniture, and
pottery, china, and glass.

For a listing of over 40,000 addresses
of antiques shops throughout the
country : www.curioscape.com.

AUCTIONS

American Pottery Exchange
Internet auctions only
www.the-apx.com
Popular ceramics; includes Lu Ray,

Russel Wright, Eva Ziesel, McCoy,
Bauer, and many more.

Christie's
20 Rockefeller Plaza
New York, NY 10020
212-636-2000
www.christies.com
Public auctions in the categories of
Contemporary Art, Twentieth-Century
Decorative Arts, American Furniture,
and Decorative Arts.

EBay
Internet auctions only
www.ebay.com
Individual sellers, quality and prices
vary, with every category of
merchandise represented.

Sotheby's
1334 York Avenue at 72nd Street
New York, NY 10021
212-606-7000
www.sothebys.com
Public auctions in Ceramics and
Glass, Furniture, and Decorative Arts;
also features auctions online.

FLEA MARKETS

Alameda Swap Meet
Located on South Alameda Blvd.
Los Angeles, CA 90021
213-233-2764
Well-known, wide selection, and it
never hurts to look; held 7 days a
week from 10 a.m. to 7 p.m. year
round, 400 vendors.

Brimfield Antique Show
Route 20
Brimfield, MA 01010
413-245-3436
www.brimfieldshow.com
Renowned as the Outdoor Antiques
Capital of the World, this show is held
for a week in the months of May, July,
and September.

Traders Village (Houston)
Eldridge Road
Houston, TX 77083
713-890-5500
Largest marketplace on the Texas Gulf
Coast, with over 800 dealers and over
60 acres of bargains. Free admission,
nominal parking fee. Open year-round
on Saturday and Sunday, from 8 a.m.
to 6 p.m.

For listings of flea markets held
throughout the country, go to
www.fleamarketguide.com.

FURNITURE AND ACCESSORIES

B & B Italia USA
U.S. Flagship location:
150 East 58th Street
New York, NY 10155
800-872-1697
www.bebitalia.it
Specializes in Bellini, Cittero, Pesce,
Scarpa, and others.

Cassina USA Inc.
155 East 56th Street
New York, NY 10022
800-770-3568
www.CassinaUSA.com
Furniture by masters Le Corbusier,
Rietveld, Frank Lloyd Wright; as well

as Phillippe Starck, Piero Lissoni, Vico
Magistretti, and more.

Design Within Reach
455 Jackson Street
San Francisco, CA 94111
800-944-2233
www.dwr.com
A consumer-friendly shop supplying
furniture from over 50 modern
designers including Alessi, Ghery,
and Knoll.

Domus Design Collection
181 Madison Avenue
New York, NY 10016
212-685-0800
www.ddcnyc.com
Wonderful selection including Pralo,
Mari, Dordoni, and many others.

Full Upright Position
1101 NW Glisan
Portland, OR 97209
800-431-5134
www.fup.com
Stocks furniture designed by Aalto,
Eames, Le Corbusier, van der Rohe,
and more.

Gansevoort Gallery
72 Gansevoort Street
New York, NY 10014
212-633-0555
www.gansevoortgallery.com
Contemporary pieces in metal,
lighting, glass, furniture, wood, and
ceramics.

Heywood-Wakefield Company
2300 SW 23rd Street
Miami, FL 33145
305-858-4240
www.heywood-wakefield.com

Exclusive furniture line, both modern and vintage pieces, and fabric selections.

Ligne Roset
U.S. Flagship location:
250 Park Avenue
New York, NY 10003
800-BY-ROSET
www.ligne-roset-usa.com
An exquisite collection of finely crafted furnishings, including glassware and ceramics by original designers with innovative shapes, textures, and materials.

Louis Poulsen Lighting
3260 Meridian Parkway
Ft. Lauderdale, FL 33331
954-349-2525
www.louispoulsen.com
Exclusive collection of tabletop, ceiling, table, and floor lighting fixtures.

Modernica
2118 East Seventh Place
Los Angeles, CA 90021
800-665-3839
www.modernica.net
Offers upholstered seating, dining tables, lighting, and modular shelving from designers of the '50s, '60s, and '70s.

MOMA Design Store
44 West 53rd Street
New York, NY 10022
800-447-6662
www.momastore.org
A finely-honed selection of furniture, lighting, kitchen, and tabletop accessories by designers including Stark, Wright, and Vasa.

Pastense
915 Cole Street, Suite 150
San Francisco, CA 94117-4315
415-242-0128
www.pastense.com
Witty collection of classic diner furnishings, including booths, tables, chairs, and stools.

Retromodern.com
805 Peachtree Street
Atlanta, GA 30308
877-724-0093
www.retromodern.com
Designs for the home from Alessi, Nono, Kartell, ICF, Knoll, and many more.

Vitra Design Museum
204 Pennsylvania Avenue, Suite B
Easton, MD 21601
410-763-7698
www.vitra.com
Offers designs for the home from Gehry, Thiel, Nelson, Eames, and others.

Vladimir Kagan Design Group
1185 Park Avenue
New York, NY 10128
212-289-0031
www.vladimirkagan.com
Both modern and vintage pieces from original designer, beginning in the '50s.

Workbench
Flagship location:
470 Park Avenue South
New York, NY 10016
800-380-2370
www.workbenchfurniture.com
Clean and functional imported Danish furniture for bedrooms and dining and living rooms.

HOME STORES

Crate & Barrel
Flagship location:
646 N Michigan Avenue
Chicago, IL 60611
800-996-9960
www.crateandbarrel.com
A wonderful source of good value furniture and accessories, including china, glass, and kitchenware.

IKEA
U.S. Flagship location:
1800 East McConnor Parkway
Schaumburg, IL 60173
www.ikea.com
Home basics at great prices, including stylish, inexpensive kitchenware.

Restoration Hardware
Flagship location:
935 Broadway
New York, NY 10011
212-260-9479
www.restorationhardware.com
Some of the funkiest home furnishings, lighting and accessories you'll find.

The Conran Shop
Bridgemarket
415 East 59th Street
New York, NY 10022
212-755-9079
www.conran.com
Home furnishings, kitchenware, tableware, and bathroom accessories.

TABLEWARE AND KITCHENWARE

Fishs Eddy
Flagship location:
889 Broadway
New York, NY 10011
212-420-2090
Overstock supplies of great '50s-style china mugs, plates, bowls, etc.

Heath Ceramics Inc.
400 Gate 5 Road
Sausalito, CA 94965
415-332-3732
www.heathceramics.com
Plates, cups, bowls, and tiles produced from original '50s designs of Edith Kiertzner Heath.

Kitchen Sink Antiques
North Carolina 27613
www.kitchensinkantiques.com
Specializes in all periods of glassware, dinnerware, kitchenware, restaurant china, and pottery.

O Group (Eva Zeisel Designs)
152 Franklin Street
New York, NY 10013
212-431-5973
www.theorangechicken.com
Deals exclusively in Eva Ziesel's designs for Hall China, Red Wing, Kipester, Zornay, and Castleton China.

Once Upon a Table
30 Crofut Street
Pittsfield, MA 01201
413-443-6622
Owner: Carol Levison
www.onceuponatable.com
A wonderful collection of European and American period kitchenware; jadeite, bakelite, FireKing, biscuit bins, and much more.

Soren Jensen
The Showplace
40 West 25th Street, Shop #130
New York, NY 10010
212-645-3871
www.jensensilver.com
Provides a collector's variety of
flatware and hollowware by Georg
Jensen and other Scandanavian
designers.

Williams-Sonoma
150 Post Street
San Francisco, CA 94108
415 362 6904
877-812-6235 for nearest store
www.williams-sonoma.com
Kitchenware and tableware.

COMPANIES WHO SUPPLIED
TABLEWARE FOR PHOTOGRAPHY

Alessi
22 Brook Street
London W1K RDF
UK
t. +44 20 7518 9091

Boom
53 Chalk Farm Road
London, NW1 8AN
UK
t. +44 20 7284 4622

Bowles and Linares
32 Hereford Road
London, W2 5AJ
UK
t. +44 20 7229 9886
f. +44 20 7313 9689

Century
68 Marylebone High Street
London, W1 3AQ
UK
t. +44 20 7487 5100
f. +44 20 7487 5168
shop@centurydesign.f9.co.uk

David Mellor Design
The Round Building & Country
Shop
Hathersage
Sheffield, S32 1BA
UK
t. +44 1433 650220
f. +44 1433 650944
davidmellor@UKOnline.co.uk

Fandango
50 Cross Street
London N1 2BA
UK
t. +44 20 7226 1777
www.fandango.uk.com

Flin Flon
138 St John Street
London, EC1V 4UA
UK
t. +44 20 7253 8849
f. +44 20 7253 8849

Freeforms
Unit 6,
58–60 Kensington Church Street
London, W8 4DB
UK
m. +44 7966 219520
www.FreeformsUK.com

Gary Grant Choice Pieces
18 Arlington Way
London, EC1R 1UY
UK
t. +44 20 7713 1122
choicepieces.co.uk

Origin 101
Gateway Arcade
Islington High Street
London, N1
UK
m. +44 7747 758 852
origin101.co.uk

Places & Spaces
30 Old Town
London, SW4
UK
t. +44 20 7498 0998

Rosenthal China (London) Ltd
c/o Josiah Wedgwood & Sons
Barlaston
Stoke-on-Trent, ST12 9ES
UK
t. +44 1782 282915
f. +44 1782 271189
rosenthal.uk@wedgwood.com

Skandium
72 Wigmore Street
London, W1H 9DL
UK
t. +44 20 7935 2077 shop
t. +44 20 7935 2088 office
f. +44 20 7224 2099
skandium@btinternet.com
www.skandium.com

Target Gallery
7 Windmill Street
London, W1P 1HF
UK
t. +44 20 7636 6295
f. +44 20 7636 6295

The Home Service
Camden Stables Market
Chalk Farm Road
London NW1 8AH
UK
m.07779793065

Themes & Variations
231 Westbourne Grove
London, W11 2SE
UK
t. +44 20 7727 5531
f. +44 20 7221 6378
go@themesandvariations.co.uk

Vessel
114 Kensington Park Road
London, W11 2PW
UK
t. +44 20 7727 8001
f. +44 20 7727 8661

ARCHITECTS AND DESIGNERS
WHOSE WORK IS FEATURED IN
THIS BOOK

Echo Design Agency
5, Sebastian Street
London, EC1V 0HD
UK
t. +44 20 7251 6990
f. +44 20 7251 6885
naomicleaver@echodesign.co.uk

VX Design
vxdesign.com

INDEX

Figures in italics indicate captions.

PICTURE CREDITS

All photographs by Thomas Stewart unless otherwise stated.

Key: **a** = above, **b** = below, **l** = left, **r** = right, **c** = centre

1 glass courtesy of Origin 101; **2** Stephen Shayler and Stephen Worth's house in Brighton; **4** above glass courtesy of Gary Grant Choice Pieces; **4** below glass courtesy of Origin 101; **10–11** plates courtesy of Themes & Variations; **12–13** Century 020 7487 5100; **14 al** Stephen Shayler and Stephen Worth's house in Brighton; **14 ar** tableware courtesy of Skandium;**14bl** Ron Wigham & Rachel Harding's apartment in London; **15** Target Gallery, London; **16–17** glass from Bowles & Linares and Vessel; **18–19** main Target Gallery, London; **20–21** David & Fiona Mellor's house in Hathersage; **22** Target Gallery, London; **23 bl** David & Fiona Mellor's house in Hathersage; **23 ar 14bl** Ron Wigham & Rachel Harding's apartment in London; **24** Century 020 7487 5100; **25 a & b** Target Gallery, London; **26** plastic set courtesy of Skandium; **27al** tableware courtesy of Alessi; **27 r** *photographer Tham Nhu-Tran*; **28** Neil Bingham's house in Blackheath, London; **29 l** *photographer Tham Nhu-Tran*; **29 r** Century 020 7487 5100; **30 l & r** *photographer Tham Nhu-Tran*; **31** Neil Bingham's house in Blackheath, London; **32–33** Stephen Shayler and Stephen Worth's house in Brighton; **34 l** *photographer Tham Nhu-Tran*; **34 c** Stephen Shayler and Stephen Worth's house in Brighton; **35** Fake London Studio; **36 ar** bowl courtesy of Gary Grant Choice Pieces **36br** Century London 020 7487 5100; **37** Target Gallery, London; **38** Stephen Shayler and Stephen Worth's house in Brighton; **39 l** vase from Freeforms; **39 r** Neil Bingham's house in Blackheath, London; **41ar** bowls courtesy of Skandium *41br photographer Tham Nhu-Tran*; **42–43** Target Gallery, London; **44 inset & 45** *photographer Tham Nhu-Tran*; **44** Target Gallery, London, *46–48 photographer Tham Nhu-Tran*; **49 a** Stephen Shayler and Stephen Worth's house in Brighton; **49 b** *photographer Tham Nhu-Tran*; **50–51** The T House in London designed by Ian Chee of VX Design, tableware left and right courtesy of Alessi; **52–55** Ron Wigham & Rachel Harding's apartment in London; **56 l** Ron Wigham & Rachel Harding's apartment in London, white dishes courtesy of Rosenthal China charger and peanut vase courtesy of Target Gallery, London; **56–57c** Ron Wigham & Rachel Harding's apartment in London, vases courtesy of Target Gallery, London; **57r** Coffee set courtesy of The Home Service, Camden Stables Market, London; **58–62** Neil Bingham's house in Blackheath, London; **62–63 main picture**, wall covering 'CANAS' by Arcadio Blasco for Gaston y Daniela, Madrid – UK distributor Abbot and Boydd, plates courtesy of Rosenthal China; **64 l** Yuen-Wei Chew's apartment in London designed by Paul Daly represented by Echo Design Agency; **64 cl & cr & 65** Rock, Victoria Embankment, London – 'think Studio 54', decanter and glasses courtesy of Gary Grant Choice Pieces, ice bucket courtesy of Flin Flon; **64 r** Neil Bingham's house in Blackheath, London; **66–67** Rock, Victoria Embankment, London – 'think Studio 54'; **67 l** ice bucket courtesy of Flin Flon; **68–73** Century London 020 7487 5100; **68** small vase courtesy of Target Gallery, wooden bowl courtesy of Origin 101; **69** ceramic dishes courtesy of Gary Grant Choice Pieces; **70 a & b** wide shallow ceramic bowl courtesy of Target Gallery **71 l & 73** ice bucket and wooden bowl courtesy of Origin 101; **71 r** dish courtesy of Gary Grant Choice Pieces; **74–79** David & Fiona Mellor's house in Hathersage; **86–91** Stephen Shayler and Stephen Worth's house in Brighton; **92–93** tableware courtesy of Skandium; **94 al** David & Fiona Mellor's house in Hathersage, coffee set courtesy of Rosenthal China; **94 b** bottles courtesy of Fandango; **96 l** lamp courtesy of Fandango, **96 l & 97** tableware courtesy of Skandium; **98** candelabra from Boom; **99** metalware courtesy of Skandium, **100–101** glass courtesy of Skandium; **101 b** Television from Places and Spaces **102–105** Fake London Studio; **102** metalware, **104 a** metal tray, **104 b** coffee pot, **105** material and **107** metal tray, all courtesy of Target Gallery, London; **106 al** *photographer Tham Nhu-Tran*; **106–107 c** Target Gallery, London; **107** Fake London Studio; **108–113** Yuen-Wei Chew's apartment in London designed by Paul Daly represented by Echo Design Agency; **109** candelabra courtesy of Rosenthal China; **110** plates courtesy of Target Gallery; **111** glasses by Bowles and Linares, from Vessel; **112–113** white tableware courtesy of Rosenthal China **114–119** The T House in London designed by Ian Chee of VX Design; **114–115** lamps courtesy of Themes and Variations, ashtrays courtesy of Alessi; **116–117 c** vases, **117 r** metal tray courtesy of Themes & Variations; **118** and ashtrays **119** courtesy of Alessi; **119** vases courtesy of Themes and Variations; **119 inset** lamp and metalware courtesy of Themes and Variations; **120–121** Target Gallery, London.